FAMINE IN THE LAND

FAMINE IN THE LAND

A PASSIONATE CALL FOR EXPOSITORY PREACHING

STEVEN J. LAWSON

MOODY PUBLISHERS
CHICAGO

Scripture quotations are taken from the *New American Standard Bible®*, Copyright © 1960, 1962, 1963, 1968, 1971, 1972, 1973, 1975, 1977 by The Lockman Foundation. Used by permission.

Scripture quotations marked NKJV are taken from the *New King James Version*. Copyright © 1982 by Thomas Nelson, Inc. Used by permission. All rights reserved.

Editor: Jim Vincent
Interior Design: Ragont Design
Cover Design: Barb Fisher, LeVan Fisher Design
Cover Photos: Lorentz Gullachsen/Getty Images and
              Ryan-Beyer/Getty Images

Library of Congress Cataloging-in-Publication Data

Lawson, Steven J.
    Famine in the land : a passionate call for expository preaching / by
Steve Lawson.
        p. cm.
    Includes bibliographical references and index.
    ISBN 978-0-8024-1121-1
    1. Preaching. 2. Bible—Homiletical use. I. Title.
BV4211.3.L39 2003
251—dc21

                                                                  2003005531

ISBN: 978-0-8024-1818-0

We hope you enjoy this book from Moody Publishers. Our goal is to provide high-quality, thought-provoking books and products that connect truth to your real needs and challenges. For more information on other books and products written and produced from a biblical perspective, go to www.moodypublishers.com or write to:

Moody Publishers
820 N. LaSalle Boulevard
Chicago, IL 60610

1 3 5 7 9 10 8 6 4 2

Printed in the United States of America

to

James Montgomery Boice

*A masterful preacher of Scripture,
a gifted author and teacher
of highest order,
and
a gracious man who accepted
my invitations to preach
when I was a young pastor
and in those visits
greatly impacted my life and ministry.*

*May the Reformation
for which he called
come.*

I solemnly charge you in the presence of God and of Christ Jesus, who is to judge the living and the dead, and by His appearing and His kingdom: preach the word; be ready in season and out of season; reprove, rebuke, exhort, with great patience and instruction. For the time will come when they will not endure sound doctrine; but wanting to have their ears tickled, they will accumulate for themselves teachers in accordance to their own desires; and will turn away their ears from the truth, and will turn aside to myths. But you, be sober in all things, endure hardship, do the work of an evangelist, fulfill your ministry.

2 TIMOTHY 4:1–5

CONTENTS

FOREWORD

SOME OBSERVERS MIGHT THINK the evangelical movement is larger and healthier today than it has ever been. After all, there are more megachurches than ever, some boasting attendance figures exceeding 20,000 people per week. Massive pep rallies, enormous songfests, and stadium-sized men's meetings have become fairly commonplace in the modern evangelical culture. Contemporary Christian music is the fastest-growing segment of the recording and broadcast industries. Christian publishing has become a major business. A few evangelical novels have even made it to the top of the New York Times best-seller lists. Evangelicals as a group would seem to have more clout and more visibility than ever.

Nonetheless, Steve Lawson says, there is a spiritual famine in the land. A dearth of biblical preaching has left the evangelical movement weak, starving for spiritual truth, and susceptible to the ravages of the enemy.

Is he right? I am convinced he is. The evidence seems overwhelming. Preaching itself is on the decline in a major way. Numerous churches—including some of the largest and best-known ones—have relegated the pulpit ministry to second-class status. The highlight of the worship service in many evangelical churches today is the music, the skits, multimedia, or a variety of other entertainments.

Where preaching is still featured, it is rarely *biblical* preaching. The trend today is toward topical messages focused on timely issues, human relationships, success and self-help, recovery from addictions, or similar themes. The typical preacher today aspires to be a motivational speaker rather than an exegete.

Steve Lawson is one of the rare and precious exceptions. He is passionate about biblical preaching, and he understands that careful biblical exposition from the pulpit is the great need of the church today. Steve's own preaching ministry is exemplary. As a faithful preacher for many years, he has been widely appreciated for the boldness, clarity, and care with which he handles Scripture. Even his writing models an exegetical approach. *Famine in the Land* is a thoroughly biblical treatment of the subject of preaching. It is a splendid digest of some of the Bible's most important and most basic instructions for preachers.

Here is a wonderful antidote for young preachers confused by all the modern emphasis on style over substance. Lawson takes us back to the Scriptures to show how *biblical* preaching is mandated and exemplified by the Bible itself. *Famine in the Land* is refreshingly straightforward and thorough. It is both challenging and encouraging.

Best of all, Steve's passion for biblical exposition is infectious. He demonstrates definitely that expository preaching *is* the biblical pattern for ministry. He also draws from the biblical text much practical advice about *how* to preach biblically.

This is a rich and invaluable resource for pastors wishing to feed their flocks as the Great Shepherd has commissioned us to do. I'm very thankful to see this book in print, and I pray that it will have a widespread impact on pastors, Bible-study leaders, evangelical ministries, and the famished members of our flocks.

John MacArthur

ACKNOWLEDGMENTS

IF YOU WERE TO ASK ME, "How long has it taken to write this book?" my answer would not be measured in terms of the recent months, but in the many years spent grasping, compiling, and living these truths on preaching. Such preparation has required time—a *lifetime*. In the truest sense, the writing of this book, *Famine in the Land*, has taken all my life.

A cloud of witnesses has surrounded me, preachers both living and dead, who bear witness to me not only to preach the Word, but to do so in a God-honoring way. In completing this book, I feel compelled to acknowledge the various people who have had a direct and positive effect upon my life, the men who have most shaped my understanding of preaching.

As a place of beginning, I wish to acknowledge three former pastors under whose biblical preaching I sat Sunday by Sunday and who have modeled for me what the pulpit is to be. Adrian Rogers of Bellevue Baptist Church in Memphis, Tennessee, W. A. Criswell of First Baptist Church in Dallas, Texas, and S. Lewis Johnson at Believer's Chapel in Dallas, Texas, modeled biblical exposition for me in my formative years. Their commitment to preaching God's inspired, inerrant, and infallible Word has molded my approach to preaching. Each one became for me living incarnations of what God had called me to do.

Further, I want to recognize former professors of mine at Dallas Theological Seminary. Haddon Robinson and Duane Litfin taught me expository preaching in the classroom, lessons that I shall never forget. Other professors at Dallas, men like Howard Hendricks, J. Dwight Pentecost, John Hannah, and Stanley Toussaint, have left their imprint upon my life. Most of all, I want to thank Roy Zuc k, who not only taught me Bible exposition, but who also asked me to write four articles on expository preaching for *Bibliotheca Sacra,* which form the basis of this book. Every page of this book, in one way or another, has been hammered on the anvil of their own expository ministries.

In addition, R. C. Sproul, one of my professors at Reformed Theological Seminary, further instructed me in the finer points of communication. Every one of his classes was filled with his passion to convey the truth of Scripture, and still remains fresh and memorable in my mind.

Moreover, I wish to express gratitude for the expository preaching of John MacArthur, pastor-teacher of Grace Community Church in Sun Valley, California. His relentless pursuit of the meaning of the biblical text and his passionate preaching of that passage with a God-centered focus has shaped my entire approach to the pulpit. This man of God has established for me, and for an entire generation, the highest standard of what biblical preaching should be.

Not all my mentors are living. Many men continue to mold me long after they have passed off the scene. I refer to the Reformers, men like Martin Luther and John Calvin; the Puritans, most especially Thomas Watson and John Owen; and other pulpit stalwarts who have followed in their trail, mighty preachers like George Whitefield, Jonathan Edwards, Charles H. Spurgeon, and, more recently, Martyn Lloyd-Jones. Reading their sermons and studying their lives has left me radically changed. The pages of this book flow out of the influence of each of these men.

In addition, I am grateful to the team at Moody Publishers, especially Mark Tobey, who believed in the message of this book, and Jim Vincent, whose skillful editing has woven this manuscript into a seamless garment for God's glory.

In the truest sense, the writing of this book *has* taken all my life. Each of the aforementioned pastors and professors, as well as luminous figures of centuries past, have directly shaped my life regarding the pulpit, a lasting influence that, I trust, will bleed through the print of this book. May God use all this for His glory and our good.

Introduction

DAYS OF DROUGHT

DR. D. MARTYN LLOYD-JONES, the famed expositor of Westminster Chapel in London, while lecturing on preaching at Westminster Theological Seminary, stated, "The most urgent need in the Christian Church today is true preaching; and as it is the greatest and the most urgent need in the Church, it is the greatest need of the world also."[1]

If the doctor's diagnosis is correct, and this writer believes it is, then a return to preaching—*true* preaching, *biblical* preaching, *expository* preaching—is the greatest need in this critical hour. If a reformation is to come to the church, it must be preceded by a reformation of the pulpit. As the pulpit goes, so goes the church.

The prophet Amos warned of a famine that would cover the land, a dearth of hearing the Word of the Lord (Amos 8:11). Theologian Walter Kaiser is among many who have declared the famine is now here, and has been here for some time: "The famine of the Word continues in massive proportions in most places in North America."[2] Indeed, we are living in such days of drought, a time when many forces are suffocating biblical preaching. Now more than ever, pastors must return to their highest calling, the divine summons to "preach the word" (2 Tim. 4:2).

What exactly is expository preaching? We are hard pressed to find a better definition than the one given by J. I. Packer in *God Has Spoken:* "The true idea of preaching is that the preacher should become a mouthpiece for his text, opening it up and applying it as a word from God to his hearers, talking only in order that the text itself may speak and be heard." Packer noted that the preacher must "[make] each point from his text in such a manner that" [quoting from the Westminster dictionary] "the hearers may discern how God teacheth it from thence."[3] This is the true nature of preaching. It is the man of God opening the *Word* of God and expounding its truths so that *voice* of God may be heard, the *glory* of God seen, and the *will* of God obeyed.

Speaking centuries ago, the Genevan Reformer John Calvin stated that preaching involves the explication of Scripture, unfolding its natural and true meaning, while making application to the life and experience of the congregation.[4] In other words, exposition involves both *explication* and *application,* or the Word carefully explained and practically related to life. Calvin further stated, "Preaching is the public exposition of Scripture by the man sent from God, in which God himself is present in judgment and in grace."[5] This strikes at the heart of what expository preaching *truly* is. It is preaching the Bible, explaining the true meaning of the Scripture in a way that conveys divine judgment if it is refused and divine grace if received. In this sense, Calvin argues, God is *unusually* present in the preaching of His Word.

This is the supernatural dynamic of expository preaching. When the Bible speaks, *God* speaks.

More recently, Merrill Unger defined biblical exposition as communicating the "real and essential meaning" of a passage of Scripture "as it existed in the mind of the particular Biblical writer and as it exists in the light of the overall context of Scripture."[6] It is, he explained, "God's Word made plain and applied to the present-day needs of the hearers." Unger added, "It is emphatically not preaching about the Bible, but preaching the Bible. 'What saith the Lord' is the alpha and omega of expository preaching. It begins in the Bible and ends in the Bible and all that intervenes springs from the Bible. In other words, expository preaching is Bible-centered preaching."[7] Or, as J. I. Packer writes, it is simply "letting texts talk."[8] *This* is what is meant by expository preaching and *this* is the dire need today.

Famine in the Land is an expansion of a four-part series originally published in *Bibliotheca Sacra* in 2001–2002.[9] Some of the material prepared for the *Bib Sac* series, omitted due to space constraints, has been restored in this book. These additions will provide a more polemic and provocative effect. The chapters themselves are expositions of the Scripture, actually modeling what they call for, namely, a God-centered message extracted from a biblical text. This text-driven approach will allow God's Word to determine the *place* expository preaching should have in the church today, as well as define *how* the Word is to be preached.

These pages are intended to fortify the allegiance of all who proclaim the Word, whether they be pastors, teachers, evangelists, seminary professors, or Bible college professors, as well as students preparing for a preaching ministry. This book is designed to rally all who are in the trenches faithfully preaching and teaching the Scripture to discern and deflect the many threats that have arisen in this present hour against expounding the full counsel of God. Likewise, it is written to encourage those in the pew who love the faithful preaching of God's Word, challenging them to support those who feed them a steady diet of the Scripture.

Famine in the Land directly addresses what, I believe, is the crying need of the hour, specifically that the modern-day pulpit be restored to her former glory of generations past, days when God's truth was fearlessly proclaimed—days when doctrinal clarity, theological precision, and heart-searching application once poured forth from pulpits.

This book goes forth with the prayer that in these days of famine across the land, the head of the church, the Lord Jesus Christ, will once again raise up godly men who will, faithfully and fearlessly, *preach the Word*. May God be pleased to grant such a powerful reformation and revival to His church for the sovereign glory of His blessed name.

Notes

1. Martyn Lloyd-Jones, *Preaching and Preachers* (Grand Rapids: Zondervan, 1971), 9.

2. Walter C. Kaiser Jr., *Revive Us Again* (Nashville: Broadman & Holman, 1999), 166.

3. J. I. Packer, *God Has Spoken* (Downers Grove, Ill.: InterVarsity, 1979), 28.

4. John H Leigh, "Calvin's Doctrine of the Proclamation of the Word and Its Significance for Today in the Light of Recent Research," *Review and Expositor* 86 (1989): 32, 34.

5. As quoted in John Blanchard, comp. *Gathered Gold* (Darlington, Del.: Evangelical Press, 1984), 238.

6. Merrill F. Unger, *Principles of Expository Preaching* (Grand Rapids: Zondervan, 1955), 33.

7. Ibid., 9.

8. As cited in Alistair Begg, *Preaching for God's Glory* (Wheaton, Ill.: Crossway, 1999), 9.

9. Steve Lawson, "The Priority of Biblical Preaching: An Expository Study of Acts 2:42–47," *Bibliotheca Sacra* 158 (April–June 2001): 198–217; "The Power of Biblical Preaching: An Expository Study of Jonah 3:1–10," *Bibliotheca Sacra* 158 (July–September 2001): 331–46; "The Pattern of Biblical Preaching: An Expository Study of Ezra 7:10 and Nehemiah 8:1–18," *Bibliotheca Sacra* 158 (October–December 2001): 451–66; "The Passion of Biblical Preaching: An Expository Study of 1 Timothy 4:13–16," *Bibliotheca Sacra* 158 (January–March 2002): 79–95. Originally published in *Bibliotheca Sacra* and is used by permission.

A nd they were continually devoting themselves to the apostles' teaching and to fellowship, to the breaking of bread and to prayer.

And everyone kept feeling a sense of awe; and many wonders and signs were taking place through the apostles. And all those who had believed were together, and had all things in common; and they began selling their property and possessions, and were sharing them with all, as any might have need. And day by day, continuing with one mind in the temple, and breaking bread from house to house, they were taking their meals together with gladness and sincerity of heart, praising God, and having favor with all the people. And the Lord was adding to their number day by day those who were being saved.

ACTS 2:42–47

"The pulpit is the throne for the Word of God."

❖ MARTIN LUTHER

1

FEAST OR FAMINE?
THE PRIORITY OF BIBLICAL PREACHING

AS THE CHURCH ADVANCES into the twenty-first century, the stress to produce booming ministries has never been greater. Influenced by corporate mergers, towering skyscrapers, and expanding economies, bigger is perceived as better, and nowhere is this "Wall Street" mentality more evident than in the church. Sad to say, pressure to produce bottom-line results has led many ministries to sacrifice the centrality of biblical preaching on the altar of man-centered pragmatism.

A new way of "doing" church is emerging. In this radical paradigm shift, exposition is being replaced with entertainment, preaching with performances, doctrine with drama, and theology with theatrics. The pulpit, once the focal point of the church, is now being overshadowed by a variety of church-growth techniques, everything from trendy worship styles to glitzy presentations and vaudeville-like pageantries. In seeking to capture the upper hand in church growth, a new wave of pastors is reinventing church and repackaging the gospel into a product to be sold to "consumers."[1]

Whatever reportedly works in one church is being franchised out to various "markets" abroad. As when gold was discovered in the foothills of northern California, so ministers are beating a path to the doorsteps of exploding churches and super-hyped conferences where the latest "strike" has been reported. Unfortunately, the newly panned gold often turns out to be "fool's gold." Not all that glitters is actually gold.

GOD'S WORK, GOD'S WAY

Admittedly, pastors can learn from growing churches and successful ministries. Yet God's work must be done God's way if it is to know God's blessing. He provides the power and He alone should receive the glory, but this will happen only when His divinely prescribed plan for ministry is followed. When people-centered schemes are followed, often imitating the world's shtick, the flesh provides the energy, and people—not God—receive the glory.

Throughout church history, preachers who have left a lasting impact on the church have known that, in the words of Michael Horton, "the regular proclamation of Christ through the close exposition of Scripture [is] more relevant in creating a worshipping and serving community than political causes, moral crusades, and entertaining services."[2] In many evangelical churches, however, the centrality of biblical exposition is being demoted to second-class status. In a strange twist, the preaching of the Cross is now foolishness, not only to the world, but also to the contemporary church. The result has been a famine of biblical preaching in our land.

This famine in pulpits across the nation reveals a loss of confidence in God's Word to perform its sacred work. While evangelicals affirm the inerrancy of Scripture, many have apparently abandoned their belief in its *sufficiency* to save and to sanctify. Rather than expounding the Word with growing vigor, many are turning to lesser strategies in an effort to resurrect dead ministries. But with each newly added novelty, the straightforward expounding of the Bible is being relegated to a secondary role, further starving the church. Doing God's work God's way requires an unwavering commitment to feeding people God's Word through relentless biblical preaching and teaching.

A PARADIGM FOR MINISTRY

With many ministries forsaking a steady diet of biblical exposition, where is an effective model to be found in which preaching and teaching God's Word is the main entree? What does it look like when a church is being served the meat of God's Word? One need look no further than to the first church in Jerusalem, born on the Day of Pentecost and firmly planted in the soil of newly converted hearts. Today's church leaders would do well to revisit this congregation and rediscover the strategy of its earliest leaders, the apostles.

After the apostle Peter boldly preached to the gathered crowd at Pentecost, three thousand souls were pierced to the heart, saved, and then baptized. In condensed form, Acts 2:42–47 portrays the potent life of this newly formed congregation. These verses contain the major components of the dynamic life of this first congregation—the apostles' teaching, fellowship, worship, prayer, service, and evangelism. Here are the six channels through which God's Spirit pulsated through believers and dramatically impacted the world around them. Each of these spiritual disciplines is critical for the health of any church that seeks to wholly honor God.

Purposefully listed first in this passage, the apostles' teaching will be the focus of this chapter, which examines the strategic place, specific pattern, and supernatural power that such teaching occupied in this first church. This study is a call to the contemporary church to make biblical preaching central, just as the apostles did two thousand years ago—to move from the present famine to a future feast. The early church experienced spiritual vitality, not because of gimmicky techniques, but because it focused on the priority of biblical teaching. Along this line, Acts 2:42–47 demonstrates the God-assigned role of the apostles' doctrine.

THE PRIMACY OF THE APOSTLES' TEACHING

Listed first in this cluster of ministries, the apostles' teaching was the chief ministry of these first church leaders. First and foremost, the apostles *taught*. More specifically, they taught *doctrine*. Their teaching ministry brought life to all the other aspects of the first church. It is no accident that teaching came first.[3] It must *always* come first. In the Christian life, precept comes before practice, doctrine before duty, and exposition before experience. As John Phillips has well stated, "Experience must always be tested by doctrine, not doctrine by experience."[4]

John Stott observed that these "new converts were not enjoying a mystical experience which led them to despise their mind or disdain theology. . . . Anti-intellectualism and the fullness of the Spirit are mutually incompatible, because the Holy Spirit is the Spirit of truth."[5] That is to say, the Holy Spirit worked mightily in this first church by leading the apostles to be prolific in their teaching ministry. Sound doctrine enriched every aspect of this church's life. Every strategy and ministry flowed from the pure fountain of biblical truth. As the chief activity of the apostles, their teaching was primary and powerfully effective, a timeless pattern that was modeled in Jesus' ministry, commanded in the Great Commission, practiced in the early church, and reinforced in the Pastoral Epistles.

MODELED IN JESUS' MINISTRY

As the apostles taught this first flock, they were following what they had seen Jesus Christ do. For more than three years they had been directly taught by Christ Himself and had witnessed His public ministry. They understood the central importance He placed on teaching. From the time Christ first called them to follow Him until His ascension, teaching was His chief occupation. No doubt His disciples-in-training noted this priority in His ministry. So central was His teaching ministry that the Twelve called Him "Teacher" (John 13:13), and He called each of them His "disciple" (Matt. 10:24–25; Luke 6:40), a word used of any learner who sat under a teacher and absorbed his teaching.[6] Such terms clearly indicate the primary place of teaching in Christ's ministry.

As Jesus launched His public ministry, He came "preaching the gospel of God" (Mark 1:14). Soon after that, He entered a synagogue in Nazareth and read from Isaiah: "The Spirit of the Lord is upon Me, because He anointed Me to preach the gospel to the poor. He has sent Me to proclaim release to the captives" (Luke 4:18). He thus claimed that His preaching fulfilled Isaiah's prophecy. When large numbers came to Him to be healed, He withdrew from them, stating, "Let us go somewhere else to the towns nearby, in order that I may preach there also" (Mark 1:38).

Nothing would deter Him from His primary ministry of preaching and teaching, not even the compassionate healing of the sick. When the multitudes came, "He began to teach them" (Matt. 5:2). Throughout His public ministry, the proclamation of God's truth remained paramount. Even the night before He was crucified, Jesus gathered His disciples in a cloistered upper room and taught them (John 13–16).

After His resurrection, the focus of Jesus' ministry remained the same. While walking on the road to Emmaus,

He appeared to two disciples and "explained to them the things concerning Himself in all the Scriptures" (Luke 24:27). When the disciples met in the Upper Room, Jesus appeared in their midst and "opened their minds to understand the Scriptures" (v. 45) regarding "all things which are written" about Him "in the Law of Moses and the Prophets and the Psalms" (v. 44). And just before Jesus was taken up into heaven, He was instructing His disciples (Acts 1:1–9).

This central thrust in Christ's ministry, namely, preaching and teaching, left a deep impression on His disciples. As the Twelve began their pastoral work, as stated in Acts 2:42, they were merely imitating what they had observed Jesus do, repeating what had been modeled before them. As they shepherded this first church in Jerusalem, they immediately began teaching, because this was what Jesus had done with them. Any other ministry priority would have been a departure from the consistent example they had seen in Christ's own ministry.

Commanded in the Great Commission

Furthermore, the apostles taught these new believers because this was what Jesus had commanded them to do. In the Great Commission issued only days earlier, Jesus had charged them: "Go therefore and make disciples of all the nations, baptizing them in the name of the Father and the Son and the Holy Spirit, teaching them to observe all that I commanded you; and lo, I am with you always, even to the end of the age" (Matt. 28:19–20).

In this authoritative mandate, their essential responsibilities—going, making disciples, baptizing, and teaching—climaxed in this last charge of "teaching," as they were commanded to indoctrinate the new believers in all He had taught them. As Jesus had instructed them, He now directed them to do the same with others. In fact, teaching is so foundational to fulfilling in the Great Commission that Jesus identified His future followers as "disciples," or learners. First and foremost, the apostles were to make *learners*—not "fellowshipers," breakers-of-bread, or prayers. Although these other spiritual disciplines of fellowshiping with each other, communing with Christ, and praying to God are undeniably important, they would become a reality only as these new followers were *first* taught the essential truths of the Christian faith. So in obedience to what Christ had commanded in the Great Commission, the apostles taught new believers.

PRACTICED IN THE EARLY CHURCH

The fact that these new believers were "*continually devoting themselves* to the apostles' teaching" (Acts 2:42, italics added) implies that the Twelve were teaching on a regular, ongoing basis. The apostles' ministry of preaching and teaching is mentioned more often than any other activity in which they were engaged (Acts 2:42; 3:11–26; 4:1–2, 8–12, 19–20, 31, 33; 5:20–21, 29–32, 42; 6:2, 4, 7–10; 7:1–53). So overwhelming is this evidence that it can be argued that Acts is primarily a record of apostolic preaching and teaching. John MacArthur concluded, "The early church sat under the teaching ministry of the apostles, whose teaching, now written on the pages of the New Testament Scriptures, is to be taught by all pastors."[7]

No matter where they were, these apostles were preaching. Whether in Solomon's temple (3:11–26; 5:20, 42), in public gatherings (4:2, 33), before the Sanhedrin (4:8–12; 5:27–32), or from house to house (5:42), they boldly taught in the name of Christ. Even in the face of life-threatening dangers, the apostles refused to be silenced, declaring, "We cannot stop speaking what we have seen and heard" (4:20). When the demands of ministry grew complex, they would not be diverted from their central task of teaching. They said, "It is not desirable for us to neglect the word of God" (6:2). Most notably, when the successful expansion of their ministry was described, it was measured in terms of spreading "the word of God" (v. 7). Similarly, when those under their teaching—men such as Stephen and Philip—were thrust into ministry, they taught the "word" with extraordinary effectiveness (7:2–50; 8:5–6, 25–35, 40). In fact, the first disciples filled all Jerusalem with their teaching (5:28). Unmistakably, the apostles' teaching was most important in the early church.

REINFORCED IN THE PASTORAL EPISTLES

The primacy of the apostles' teaching was a central theme in the Pastoral Epistles. The apostle Paul encouraged Timothy and Titus to devote themselves to the ministry of preaching and teaching God's Word. The first duty with which Paul charged his young associate, Timothy, was to "instruct" the church about proper doctrine (1 Tim. 1:3), which is "the pillar and support of the truth" (3:15). Timothy was to be "constantly nourished on the words of faith and of the sound doctrine" (4:6) and to "prescribe and teach these things" (v. 11). He was to "give attention to the public reading of Scripture, to exhortation and teaching" (v. 13), never neglecting his "spiritual gift" of teaching (v. 14). He must "take pains with" and "be absorbed in" his teaching, paying "close attention" to his "teaching" (vv. 15–16). All ministers, Paul wrote, must "work hard at preaching and teaching" (5:17), instructing (6:17), and guarding the truth (v. 20).

In 2 Timothy, Paul reinforced this theme with his young son in the faith. Timothy was to "retain the standard of sound words" (2 Tim. 1:13), "guard" it (v. 14), and "entrust" it to others (2:2). He was to "remind" others of the truth (v. 14), be "handling accurately the word of truth" (v. 15), and be "able to teach" (v. 24). Solemnly charged before God, Timothy must "preach the word" "with great . . . instruction" (4:2).

Paul also encouraged Titus to minister God's Word. All pastors must "be able both to exhort in sound doctrine and to refute those who contradict" (Titus 1:9). He told Titus, "Speak the things which are fitting for sound doctrine" (2:1). Paul charged him, "These things speak and exhort and reprove with all authority. Let no one disregard you" (v. 15).

Thus, in these three Pastoral Epistles, the apostle Paul affirmed the *primary* responsibility of the ministry, namely, to effectively disseminate the apostles' teaching.

THE FOREMOST RESPONSIBILITY

Biblical preaching must *always* occupy the leading place of influence in the life of any church. At the core of any healthy congregation is a vibrant exposition of God's Word. Unfortunately, though, many pastors are turning away from the central role of expository preaching and doctrinal teaching. But in so doing, they fail to realize that new converts, first and foremost, need to be taught God's truth. As a result, many other things are competing with—and even replacing—the primary role of biblical preaching in the church. Christian concerts, drama, pageants, festivals, musicals, talk shows, and religious movies are establishing a greater foothold in the life of the contemporary church. *Some* of these activities *may* have a place in the church, but they must never compete with nor overshadow the Spirit-energized proclamation of God's Word within a church.

In diagnosing the ills of emphasis on these auxiliary methods, Martyn Lloyd-Jones lamented, "All this at best is secondary, very often, not even secondary, often not worthy of a place at all. . . . The primary task of the Church and of the Christian minister is the preaching of the Word of God."[8] He echoed the words of the chief pastoral voice of the Great

Awakening, Jonathan Edwards, who declared, "The primary importance of the pastor is to be an expository preacher."[9]

Evangelical churches desperately need to return to the primacy of the apostles' teaching. Preaching is the foremost responsibility of the preacher and the church.

THE PATTERN OF THE APOSTLES' TEACHING

Since the apostles' teaching was so primary, what exactly did they teach? What was the content of their doctrine?

They expounded the pure truth of divine revelation, firmly grounding new converts in the essential tenets of the Christian faith. At least three things may be noted about their teaching ministry: It was rooted in the Old Testament, focused on Jesus Christ, and centered on doctrinal instruction.

ROOTED IN THE OLD TESTAMENT

Peter's sermon on the Day of Pentecost demonstrates how heavily the apostles drew on the Old Testament Scriptures in their teaching (Acts 2:14–36). Replete with biblical quotations, this first Christian message was a biblical exposition of several key Old Testament passages (Joel 2:28–32; Pss. 16:8–11; 110:1). Even when Peter later stood before the Sanhedrin, he cited the Old Testament (Acts 4:6–10; cf. Ps. 118:22; Isa. 28:16).

In turn, the new believers who sat under the apostles' teaching repeatedly used the Old Testament. For example, after Peter and John were released by the Sanhedrin, they returned to the believers and reported what God had done (Acts 4:23). In response, the believers spontaneously lifted their voices to God in prayer (4:24–31), quoting several Old Testament passages (Exod. 20:11; Pss. 2:1–2; 146:6).

Stephen, one of the early disciples who studied under the apostles' teaching (Acts 6:3, 5), also addressed the Sanhedrin (7:2–53), quoting extensively from the Old Testament. The following list includes only a few of the many citations and allusions Stephen made to the Old Testament in his sermon.

STEPHEN'S MESSAGE		OLD TESTAMENT REFERENCE
ACTS	**7:3**	Genesis 12:1
	7:5	Genesis 12:7; 17:8
	7:6	Genesis 15:13
	7:7	Exodus 3:12
	7:18	Exodus 1:8
	7:27–29	Exodus 2:14–15
	7:30–34	Exodus 3:1–10
	7:37	Deuteronomy 18:15, 18
	7:40	Exodus 32:1, 23
	7:42–43	Amos 5:25–27
	7:49–50	Isaiah 66:1–2

Having grown up as a Jew, Stephen no doubt knew the Old Testament well, but he was almost surely taught by the apostles. As a believer in Christ, he told the Sanhedrin that the Old Testament prophets "announced the coming of the Righteous One" (Acts 7:52).

Philip, another disciple apparently taught by the apostles (6:3, 5), showed great competence in handling the Old Testament. For example, when the Ethiopian eunuch asked him to explain Isaiah 53:7–8, Philip immediately gave the true interpretation (Acts 8:25–35). This precise handling of Scripture unmistakably argues for the foundational role of the Old Testament in the apostles' teaching. Thus, the Old Testament was the underlying foundation of their doctrine.

RIVETED ON JESUS CHRIST

The chief subject of the apostles' teaching ministry was the words and works of Jesus Christ. For more than three years, they had been eyewitnesses of His perfect life and keen students of His prolific teaching. They were so closely associated with Him that others noted that they "[had] been with Jesus" (4:13). Understandably, their apostolic teaching focused on the Lord—His life, deity, discourses, parables, promises, conversations, invitations, denunciations, death, resurrection, ascension, and enthronement. It has been noted, "The words and works of Jesus . . . formed the burden of the Apostles' message."[10]

Peter's sermon on the Day of Pentecost (2:14–36) was a concise, cohesive presentation of the Lord Jesus Christ, outlining His life and miracles (v. 22), death (v. 23), resurrection (vv. 24–32), and exaltation (vv. 33–36). In the Upper Room, He had promised the apostles He would send the Holy Spirit, who would enable them to remember all He had taught them. He assured them, "But the Helper, the Holy Spirit, whom the Father will send in My name, He will teach you all things, and bring to your remembrance all that I said to you" (John 14:26). Now, in fulfillment of that promise, the Spirit had come and enabled them to remember Christ's many words. So when the apostles taught, they were "teaching in this name" (Acts 5:28), that is, speaking "in the name of Jesus" (v. 40). The apostles' teaching clearly focused on the life, ministry, and teaching of Jesus Christ.

REVEALED WITH DOCTRINAL INSTRUCTION

Also, the apostles' teaching clarified many of the great themes of the Old Testament. *Didache,* the Greek word for "teaching," referred to the content of their message, or the body of truth emanating from their teaching. Occurring thirty times in the New Testament, *didache* often refers to the fixed body of doctrine as taught by the apostles to the church. In the earthly ministry of Jesus, *didache* referred to the content of His preaching and teaching (Mark 1:22, 27; 11:18; 12:38), including His many discourses, such as the Sermon on the Mount (Matt. 7:28), as well as His exposition of the Law (22:33).[11] In the book of Acts, *didache* included the apostles' exposition of Jesus' words. This testimony of the apostles to Jesus Christ became known as "the apostles' teaching" (Acts 2:42), "the teaching of the Lord" (13:12), or "this new teaching" (17:19).[12]

As the church grew, the apostles' teaching was identified as "the whole message of this Life" (5:20) and "the whole purpose of God" (20:27). It included the Old Testament, the life and teachings of Jesus Christ, and the rich doctrinal teachings to be recorded in the New Testament. Everett Harrison called the apostles' teaching a "well-defined pattern of instruction for new converts." He added,

> It must have included the high points of Jesus' life and works; His ethical teaching, such as is enshrined in the Sermon on the Mount; an appreciation of the Old Testament prophetic background for His ministry, such as He imparted to the eleven after His resurrection; a digest of obligations toward one another, especially in the family relationship and toward those outside the fold; and a warning about the possibility of persecution and the inroads of false teaching. . . . They needed . . . insight into the epochal character of the new age into which they had entered because of Christ's finished work and the advent of the Spirit.[13]

Thus, the apostles' teaching covered many facets of divinely revealed truth, including historical truth (Jesus' life and work), ethical truth (practical application), prophetic truth (Old Testament background), theological truth (systematized doctrine), domestic truth (mutual responsibilities), and eschatological truth (the age to come). The apostles' teaching was God's plan of redemption centered on the Lord Jesus Christ: the facts that (1) He is the focal point of all God's purposes in the earth, (2) people can know Him and how to live for Him, and (3) His kingdom is coming. Far from a mere elementary course in Christianity, the apostles' teaching included the all-encompassing truths recorded in the Old Testament, the mind-expanding, life-changing words spoken by Christ, and the enriched doctrine elaborated on by the apostles in greater detail.

PABULUM IN THE PULPIT

Tragically, most of what passes for biblical preaching today falls woefully short of apostolic standards. Many pastors seem content to dole out pabulum to spiritual babies instead of teaching the full counsel of God. Many evangelical ministers have succumbed to delivering secular-sounding, motivational pep talks aimed at soothing the felt needs of restless church shoppers or, worse, salving the guilty consciences of unregenerate church members. Rather than expounding the depths of God's Word, many Bible-believing ministers have chosen the path of least resistance, content to scratch the surface of shallow souls and tickle the ears of languid listeners. The result is congregations are starving—even though many of the famished may not be aware of it—settling for sickly sweet, yet totally inadequate, spiritual pabulum.

If people are to be brought to saving faith in Christ and are to mature spiritually, pastors must teach a comprehensive biblical message that is rooted in both the Old and New Testaments, focused on Christ, and full of doctrinal instruction. *Where* are such pulpits today?

THE PURITY OF THE APOSTLES' TEACHING

The apostles did not espouse their own self-styled speculations; their teaching was the authoritative message of God Himself. As such, it was the highest standard in the church, the unchanging plumb line by which all else was measured. Three facts should be noted about the authority of their teaching.

DECLARED AS GOD'S TRUTH

As God's chosen mouthpieces, the apostles were the divinely appointed means through whom His truth was communicated. Their message was God's message, not their own; therefore, it came with divine authority. "Before He ascended, He delegated this authority to the apostles, who spoke in His name," noted commentator Simon Kistemaker.[14] The Greek word for "apostle" (*apostolos*) means "a messenger, one sent on a mission"[15] According to the *Theological Dictionary of the New Testament,* "It always denotes a man who is sent, and sent with full authority."[16] Therefore, an *apostolos* was dispatched as an official envoy with authority to speak on behalf of the sender. In the New Testament, the word refers primarily to the twelve men whom Christ designated to represent Him in transmitting His message both to the world and the church. To these selected representatives Christ gave His authority to speak His message. F. F. Bruce aptly remarks, "The apostolic teaching . . . was authoritative because it was the teaching of the Lord communicated through the apostles."[17]

The importance of the apostolic office is seen in the way Judas's replacement was chosen (Acts 1:21–26). Certain requirements had to be met in order to be an apostle. First, an apostle had to have been present with Christ from the earliest days of His ministry and to have been an eyewitness of

His resurrection (vv. 21–22). This requirement ensured his full exposure to, as well as deep conviction about, the Lord's life, teaching, and resurrection. Second, an apostle had to be one whom the Lord Himself had specifically appointed to this office (vv. 24–25). Even among the many people who had heard His instruction and seen His post-resurrection appearances, the Lord did not choose all of them to be apostles. Only a limited number were chosen to be His apostles; through these men, uniquely qualified and sovereignly selected, He would speak with divine authority.

In this God-designated role, the apostles spoke divine revelation to the church. Thus, the church's ministry would be "built on the foundation of the apostles and prophets" (Eph. 2:20). The apostles' teaching became the unchanging, unshifting bedrock of the church. As Paul wrote, "For no man can lay a foundation other than the one which is laid, which is Jesus Christ" (1 Cor. 3:11). The apostles' teaching singularly points to Jesus Christ, the only true foundation for any New Testament church.[18] Because a foundation can be laid only once—at the beginning of a construction project—the apostles' teaching was given initially at the "groundbreaking" of the first-century church, not to be reissued with each subsequent generation. Throughout the present church age, all ministries must build on this same unchanging body of truth, the apostles' teaching, which was "once for all delivered to the saints" (Jude 3).

DOCUMENTED BY GOD'S POWER

How did the early church know with certainty that these men were true apostles? How did believers have the assurance that these men spoke with divine authority? "Many wonders and signs were taking place through the apostles" (Acts 2:43). God authenticated the apostles as His representatives by giving them supernatural power to perform miracles (Matt. 10:1; 2 Cor. 12:12). Each miracle confirmed that they were men of God who spoke the truth of God. "Wonders" refers to the amazement people experienced when they witnessed these miracles of God performed by the Twelve. "Signs" point to God's power behind the miracles, authenticating that the apostles spoke as God's messengers, bearing His eternal truth, the Word of God.

Wrought by the Holy Spirit, such mighty works were performed through the apostles (Acts 2:43; 5:12–16), as well as their associates (6:8), to validate that their message was from God. Such signs passed off the scene by the end of the first century, but the power of God to change lives today brings unmistakable authentication to the divine authority of the message preached.

DETAILED IN GOD'S WORD

By the end of the first century, the apostles' teaching was permanently recorded in the twenty-seven books of the New Testament. Every canonical book was either written by an apostle or backed by an apostle. Most of Paul's epistles and Peter's two epistles, for example, begin with an affirmation of the writer's apostleship. Preserved in the pages of the New Testament, the apostles' teaching remains the highest standard of authority and only source of doctrine in the church today. Everyone and everything in the church must yield to that New Testament authority. Every decision, direction, practice, ministry, attitude, and motive must be brought into conformity with their instruction.

The *living* Word, Jesus Christ, presently rules His church through His *written* Word, the Scriptures. Thus, everything must be brought into alignment with God's Word.

To Be Spoken with Authority

Such authoritative preaching is desperately needed in the church today. While many churches are catering to the whims of a self-indulgent generation, all who stand before congregations must hold forth the unchanging standard of the apostles' teaching and confront each listener with the unchanging truth of God's Word. The sovereign rule of God in the lives of His people will be realized to the extent that His Word is proclaimed authoritatively and embraced willingly by those who hear it.

With words that apply to all preachers today, Paul charged Titus, "These things speak and exhort and reprove with all authority. Let no one disregard you" (Titus 2:15). True biblical preaching is authoritative in nature and boldly proclaims God's Word without compromise or apology.

The preacher is not to offer suggestions, or options to be accepted or rejected, but is to issue authoritative commands from God's Word which are to be kept and obeyed. In a day when so many preachers have cowered into being men-pleasers, where are such authoritative preachers today?

THE PASSION FOR THE APOSTLES' TEACHING

How was the apostles' teaching received? As the early-church believers gathered together, they had an unquenchable thirst and consuming appetite to be fed God's truth. John Stott has noted of the early believers: "They sat at the apostles' feet, hungry to receive instruction, and they persevered in it."[19] Of the first congregation described in Acts 2, Luke wrote that they were "continually devoting themselves to the apostles' teaching" (v. 42). These spiritual babies—*all* three thousand of them—were constantly coming to the apostles to be fed spiritual truth. There was no need for gospel gimmicks or spiritual sideshows to entice them to come, for these starving souls were craving the pure milk of the Word.

DESIRED BY HUNGRY HEARTS

Consider how the early-church believers "were continually devoting themselves to the apostles' teaching." The verb form of "devoted," *proskartereo,* means "a steadfast and single-minded fidelity to a certain course of action."[20] This colorful word is a compound in which the verb *kartereo* is joined with a prefix (*pros*) that serves to intensify the action. *Kartereo* means "to be strong, steadfast, also to do something persistently in the face of opposition,"[21] and *pros* means "to be hard by, near, at." The compound, then, describes desiring something intensely, or aggressively pursuing a desired object. This word is also used to describe the strong devotion and singular desire of the one hundred twenty who had gathered in the Upper Room for prayer after Christ's ascension (1:14). Later this verb was used to characterize the apostles' resolutely committing themselves to prayer and the ministry of the Word (6:4). In 2:42, the verb depicts the unwavering desire of these new believers to be fed God's Word by the apostles. This intense desire for the Word "expresses one aspect of the power and vitality of primitive Christianity."[22]

Regarding this spiritual hunger, pastor and author Kent Hughes noted, "Where the Spirit reigns, a love for God's Word reigns. . . . When the Spirit reigns, God's people *continually* devote themselves to the study of His Word."[23] Martyn Lloyd-Jones wrote of the believer's desire for the Word of God: "Wanting to listen to the Word is inevitable if men and women are born again and have become Christians. A babe . . . has an instinct for milk. He wants it! . . . He is alive and wants the mother's milk, and rightly so. The point is clear. One simply cannot be a Christian and have no desire for a knowledge of this truth—it is impossible."[24]

The first church intensely hungered for the apostles' teaching because they were genuinely converted. This is *normative* Christianity!

DESIGNED FOR GROWING LIVES

The apostles' teaching was designed to nourish the faith of new believers. Those who "were continually devoting themselves to the apostles' teaching" (2:42) were also those who had previously received Peter's word unto salvation and were baptized (note v. 41). Thus, all who believed were baptized, were added to the fellowship of believers, and welcomed the apostles' teaching. They were continually coming to the apostles to be instructed in God's truth. These first gatherings of the church were designed primarily for edifying believers, not for evangelizing unbelievers. Of course, they were reaching out to the unsaved, for "the Lord was adding to their number day by day those who were being saved" (v. 47). But this "evangelism explosion" was the *result* of their teaching, not the stated *purpose* of it. They gathered for edification; they scattered for evangelism.

The primary focus of their corporate worship gatherings was for building up the believers, not for reaching seekers. When this priority becomes reversed and the church meets primarily to save the lost, the apostles' teaching soon becomes compromised and diluted.

WHERE'S THE BEEF?

The contemporary church seems bent on presenting a non-offensive, felt-need message, which is a sad departure from the model presented in Acts. Delivering a watered-down, man-centered message only retards the spiritual hunger of true believers for the meat of God's Word. Instead of serving a full-course meal of God's truth, many evangelical pastors have only prolonged this low spiritual desire by offering the spiritual junk food of human philosophies and worldly thinking. Such spiritual junk food, full of "all kinds of artificial preservatives and . . . unnatural substitutes," wrote Walter Kaiser, has resulted in "theological and biblical malnutrition . . . and a worldwide spiritual famine [due to] the absence of any genuine proclamation of the Word of God."[25]

Tragically, many pastors today are catering *to* their people, sometimes under the guise of reaching lost people, rather than catering to them *with* the steak of Scripture. Pastors must avoid this well-intentioned but misdirected trend. They must focus on filling the pulpit, not the building.

When they preach, men of God must earnestly pray for the power of the Holy Spirit to create an unquenchable appetite for the Word in the hearts of believers. Spiritual leaders must fervently pray for the spiritual condition of their flocks, asking God to expose any sin that is choking out their hunger for God's Word (1 Peter 2:1–3). Preachers must once again deliver the truth, the *whole* truth, and *nothing but* the truth to eager hearts who wait to be fed the unsearchable riches of Christ. Anything less is compromise.

THE POTENCY OF THE APOSTLES' TEACHING

Can a church actually grow under a steady diet of biblical exposition? Can biblical preaching truly stimulate the growth of the church? Of course! The apostles' teaching greatly enriched the spiritual life of this first congregation as well as expanded their numbers. Never an end in itself, God's truth is always a means to a greater end, namely, leading God's people into genuine worship, personal maturity, spiritual service, and evangelistic outreach. Acts 2:42–47 spells out the multifaceted impact of the apostles' teaching.

ENERGIZED FELLOWSHIP

As these new believers grew in the truth, they grew in the Lord, and, in turn, they grew closer to each other. Forged together on the anvil of God's truth, their relationships in Christ were shaped and molded through their commonly held commitment to the teaching of the apostles. "They were continually devoting themselves to the apostles' teaching and to fellowship" (2:42). These two activities—the apostles' teaching and fellowship—are closely related, suggesting that the apostles' biblical preaching directly impacted the quality of the new believers' personal relationships. *Koinonia,* the Greek word translated "fellowship," means "association, communion, fellowship, close relationship."[26] It denotes "the unanimity and unity brought about by the Spirit."[27]

These new believers who had come to saving faith in Jesus Christ also came to understand that they were brothers and sisters in God's eternal family. The more they learned about their jointly held relationship with Christ, the closer, deeper, and richer was their fellowship in Him. As God's Word purged and purified their hearts, the quality of their love for each other grew even stronger. Thus, the apostles' teaching breathed life into their fellowship. So it will be today: A *Word-fed* church will be a *fellowshiping* church.

ELEVATED WORSHIP

As they were "continually devoting themselves to the apostles' teaching," the early-church believers were also engaged in "the breaking of bread" (2:42). Regarding their early expressions of worship, F. F. Bruce commented, "The 'breaking of bread' probably denotes more than the regular taking of food together: the regular observance of what came to be called the Lord's Supper seems to be in view."[28] As they were taught the rich truths about Christ's finished work on the cross, their worship experience at the Lord's Table intensified. The deeper they dug into the Word, the higher their hearts soared in fervent worship.

Never occurring in an intellectual vacuum, authentic praise and worship is always a heartfelt response to biblical truth. When Jesus said, "God is spirit, and those who worship Him must worship in spirit and truth" (John 4:24), He meant that genuine worship occurs when a believer responds inwardly to God's truth. In other words, theology leads to doxology. Biblical truth ignites hearts and enflames lives with a fervent, passionate love for God.

The more truth about God one learns and personally applies, the more clearly he or she will see, submit to, and worship Him. Noting this inseparable link, Paul wrote, "Let the word of Christ richly dwell within you, with all wisdom teaching and admonishing one another with psalms and hymns and spiritual songs, singing with thankfulness in your hearts to God" (Col. 3:16). A *Word-filled* church will be a *worshiping* church.

EMPOWERED PRAYERS

Those who "were continually devoted to the apostles' teaching" were also committed "to prayer" (Acts 2:42). Bruce explains, "As for the prayers in which they participated, the primary reference is no doubt to their own appointed seasons for united prayer, although we know that the apostles also attended the Jewish prayer services in the temple (cf. 3:1)."[29] This suggests that the apostles' teaching ignited a passion for prayer. That is the potency of true teaching. The more believers learn about God, the more they recognize their dependency on Him in prayer.

Christ had given specific instructions about the right attitude in prayer, as well as the right approach and the right agenda (Matt. 6:1–14). Teaching the apostles to be steadfast in prayer, Jesus said believers should always be asking, seeking, and knocking (7:7–11). He taught them to pray like a persistent friend (Luke 11:5–10), a hungry son (11:11–13), and a needy widow (18:1–8), bringing their requests to God in Jesus' name (John 14:13–14). Undoubtedly the apostles' teaching included what Jesus said about prayer as they led these first believers to intercede fervently (Acts 3:1; 4:24–31; 12:5, 12).

The same will be true today. Biblical preaching should always lead to bold praying. These go together like the two sides of a coin. As the Word goes out, prayer should go up. A *preaching* church will be a *praying* church.

ENRICHED SERVICE

As the new Christians received the apostles' teaching, they "were together, and had all things in common; and they began selling their property and possessions and were sharing them with all, as anyone might have need" (2:44–45). Regarding this new love for each other, C. K. Barrett noted, "Holding all things in common meant that owners sold their property. . . . Luke is describing a state that persisted for some time."[30] Their biblical preaching generated great concern, compassion, and commitment in their hearts for each other. Jesus had taught His disciples to share their possessions with those in need (Matt. 5:42). He taught them that they could not serve God *and* material possessions, for life does not consist in the possessions one owns (6:19–34). In the parable of the good Samaritan, Jesus commanded them to love their neighbors by meeting others' needs (Luke 10:30–37). The apostles' preaching no doubt expounded Jesus' words about loving and serving one another. As a result genuine displays of love immediately flowed from the believers' hearts for each other. Truth called for their mutual love, which they freely gave. It is no different today. A *learning* church will be a *loving* church.

EXPANDED JOY

The apostles' teaching also sparked an atmosphere of contagious joy. "Day by day continuing with one mind in the temple, and breaking bread from house to house, they were taking their meals together with gladness and sincerity of heart" (Acts 2:46). Of their contagious fellowship, Barrett wrote, "The meals referred to . . . were not weekly celebrations of the Lord's resurrection but, much more probably, the necessary daily meals, which the believers took in common."[31] The preaching of the apostles, which magnified the grace of the Lord Jesus Christ, ignited an explosive joy that spread to all, as they met from house to house.

When received by faith, God's Word always produces joy, filling hearts with gladness. Jesus said, "These things I have spoken to you, that My joy may be in you, and that your joy may be made full" (John 15:11). Far from being boring, God's Word, when preached and received, instills great exuberance. A *Word-filled* church will be a *joy-filled* church.

ENFLAMED EVANGELISM

The apostles' teaching resulted in the conversion of many individuals. As the Christians grew in their faith, they shared the gospel. They experienced "favor with all the people. And the Lord was adding to their number day by day those who were being saved" (Acts 2:47). Flowing into the lives of these new believers, God's Word was then shared with those who were without Christ, and this resulted in the daily conversion of lost souls. Like water rushing through a pipe, the apostles' teaching was pouring *into* these early believers and then *through* them into the lives of others. Evangelism flourished because the believers were strong in the written Word. With a growing confidence, they shared the good news of Christ with those around them. The apostles' exposition ignited an evangelism explosion. A *Word-centered* church will be a *witnessing* church.

HOW SHALL WE THEN PREACH?

Do evangelicals still have confidence in the preaching of God's Word to create such positive responses? In the first church, these healthy spiritual dynamics—fellowship, worship, prayer, service, joy, and evangelism—were all enriched by the apostles' teaching. And so it must be today. God's Word proclaimed in the power of the Holy Spirit is still powerful to produce the same supernatural effect.

Acts 2:42–47 headlines the priority of biblical preaching. The apostles' teaching ignited this first congregation, and it will do the same today in churches that are committed to biblical exposition. Listed first in the ministry activities of this initial flock, the apostles' teaching was the driving dynamic in this first congregation, the catalyst that stimulated their spiritual growth.

J. Dwight Pentecost, professor emeritus of Bible exposition at Dallas Theological Seminary, was asked what advice he would give seminary graduates going into the pastorate. He gave an answer that needs to be carefully heeded, not only by young men entering the ministry, but also by seasoned preachers and experienced teachers:

> *The great need across evangelicalism is exposition of the Scriptures. I sense there is a departure from that, even among some of our own grads, who are entertaining the people, giving the people what they want, whereas we are called to teach the Word. It is the Word that is the power of God to salvation, it is the Word that is*

the power for Christian living, and I would want them to make the Word of God the center of their ministry. It may not be popular, it may not build mega-churches, but it will fulfill that to which they are called upon to do in ministry.[32]

Churches today must return to the primacy of preaching God's Word. May God raise up a new generation of biblical expositors who, like those in the early church, are supremely committed to the unashamed proclamation of the apostles' teaching. Now more than ever, may they *preach the Word!*

Notes

1. For a broader discussion of this issue, see the following books: Alister McGrath, *Evangelicalism and the Future of Christianity* (Downers Grove, Ill.: InterVarsity, 1995); Mark Noll, *The Scandal of the Evangelical Mind* (Grand Rapids: Eerdmans, 1994); and David Wells, *No Place for Truth: Or Whatever Happened to Evangelical Theology?* (Grand Rapids: Eerdmans, 1993).

2. Michael Horton, "James Montgomery Boice: Servant of the Word," *Modern Reformation* 9 (September–October 2000): 10.

3. James Montgomery Boice, *Acts: An Expositional Commentary* (Grand Rapids: Baker, 1997), 56.

4. John Phillips, *Exploring Acts* (Chicago: Moody, 1986), 1:61.

5. John R. W. Stott, *The Message of Acts* (Downers Grove, Ill.: InterVarsity, 1990), 82.

6. Dietrich Müller, "Disciple," in *New International Dictionary of New Testament Theology*, ed. Colin Brown (Grand Rapids: Zondervan, 1978), 1:487–90.

7. John MacArthur Jr., *Acts 1–12*, MacArthur New Testament Commentary (Chicago: Moody, 1994), 83.

8. D. Martyn Lloyd-Jones, *Preaching and Preachers* (Grand Rapids: Zondervan, 1971), 19.

9. Ralph Turnbull, *Jonathan Edwards: The Preacher* (Grand Rapids: Baker Book House, 1958), 114.

10. William Neil, *The Acts of the Apostles,* New Century Bible Commentary (Grand Rapids: Eerdmans, 1973), 81.

11. Klaus Wegenast, "didache," *New International Dictionary of New Testament Theology*, ed. Colin Brown (Grand Rapids: Zondervan, 1986), 3:769. (I have shown all Greek words in their transliterated form because of their common usage and usage by the reader. All Hebrew words are shown with the Hebrew alphabet.)

12. Ibid., 770.

13. Everett F. Harrison, *Acts: The Expanding Church* (Chicago: Moody, 1975), 65.

14. Simon Kistemaker, *Exposition of the Acts of the Apostles,* New Testament Commentary (Grand Rapids: Baker, 1990), 110.

15. G. Abbott-Smith, *A Manual Greek Lexicon of the New Testament* (Edinburgh: T & T Clark, 1994), 55.

16. Karl Heinrich Rengstorf, *"apostolos,"* in *Theological Dictionary of the New Testament,* ed. Gerhard Kittel, trans. and ed. Geoffrey W. Bromiley (Grand Rapids: Eerdmans, 1964), 1:421.

17. F. F. Bruce, *The Book of the Acts,* New International Commentary on the New Testament (Grand Rapids: Baker, 1984), 73.

18. Boice, *Acts: An Expositional Commentary,* 56.

19. Stott, *The Message of Acts,* 82.

20. Richard N. Longnecker, "The Acts of the Apostles," in *The Expositor's Bible Commentary* (Grand Rapids: Eerdmans, 1973), 9:289.

21. Ulrich Falkenroth and Colin Brown, "Patience, Steadfastness, Endurance," in *New International Dictionary of New Testament Theology,* 2:64.

22. Walter Grundmann, *"proskartereo,"* in *Theological Dictionary of the New Testament* (1965), 3:619.

23. R. Kent Hughes, *Acts: The Church Afire* (Wheaton, Ill.: Crossway, 1996), 47–48 (italics his).

24. D. Martyn Lloyd-Jones, *Authentic Christianity* (Wheaton, Ill.: Crossway, 2000), 1:105–6.

25. Walter C. Kaiser, *Toward an Exegetical Theology* (Grand Rapids, Baker, 1981), 7–8.

26. Walter Bauer, William F. Arndt, and F. Wilbur Gingrich, *A Greek-English Lexicon of the New Testament and Other Early Christian Literature,* 2d ed., rev. F. Wilbur Gingrich and Frederick W. Danker (Chicago: University of Chicago, 1979), 439.

27. Johannes Schattenmann, "Fellowship," in *New International Dictionary of New Testament Theology,* 1:439.

28. Bruce, *The Book of Acts,* 73.

29. Ibid.

30. C. K. Barrett, *A Critical and Exegetical Commentary on the Acts of the Apostles,* International Critical Commentary (Edinburgh: Clark, 1998), 169.

31. Ibid., 170.

32. Kelley M. Mathews, "An Interview with Dr. J. Dwight Pentecost," *Dallas Connection,* winter 2000, 2.

N ow the word of the Lord came to Jonah the second time, saying, "Arise, go to Nineveh the great city and proclaim to it the proclamation which I am going to tell you." So Jonah arose and went to Nineveh according to the word of the Lord. Now Nineveh was an exceedingly great city, a three days' walk. Then Jonah began to go through the city one day's walk; and he cried out and said, "Yet forty days and Nineveh will be overthrown."

Then the people of Nineveh believed in God; and they called a fast and put on sackcloth from the greatest to the least of them. When the word reached the king of Nineveh, he arose from his throne, laid aside his robe from him, covered himself with sackcloth, and sat on the ashes. And he issued a proclamation and it said, "In Nineveh by the decree of the king and his nobles: Do not let man, beast, herd, or flock taste a thing. Do not let them eat or drink water. But both man and beast must be covered with sackcloth; and let men call on God earnestly that each may turn from his wicked way and from the violence which is in his hands. Who knows, God may turn and relent, and withdraw His burning anger so that we shall not perish."

When God saw their deeds, that they turned from their wicked way, then God relented concerning the calamity which He had declared He would bring upon them. And He did not do it.

JONAH 3:1–10

*"We cannot play at preaching.
We preach for eternity."*

❖ CHARLES HADDON SPURGEON

2

THE NEED OF THE HOUR
THE POWER OF BIBLICAL PREACHING

MUCH OF EVANGELICAL PREACHING has become increasingly impotent, and sadly, too few realize it. Like Samson from whom the Spirit departed without his knowing it, many pastors seem to have little awareness that God's power has vanished from their once-dynamic pulpits. Rather than preaching with renewed fervor, they are preoccupied with pouring their energies into secondary strategies, such as pursuing the latest church-growth programs, alternative worship styles, and corporate marketing plans to build their churches. While *some* of these augmentations *may* have a secondary place in the church, the crying need of the hour is for divine power to be restored to evangelical pulpits.[1]

At the heart of this crisis is a lost confidence in God's power to use His Word. While many hold to the inerrancy of Scripture, some pastors seem unconvinced of its sufficiency when preached to bring about God's desired results. They reason that biblical preaching is outdated and irrelevant. In some churches drama, dialogue, film clips, and similar means are taking the place of solid Bible exposition. At best, these alternate means of conveying truth are inferior to biblical preaching; at worst, they are hazardous to expositiory preaching. But these lesser means of communicating biblical truth must always take a backseat to truly biblical expository preaching, which remains to this day the supreme avenue that God ordained for conveying His Word.

Pastors would do well to revisit the ministries of God's servants in the Scriptures and heed their examples as proclaimers of God's Word. One man worthy of attention is the prophet Jonah.

ONE MAN, ONE MESSAGE, ONE METHOD

The extraordinary results of Jonah's preaching may be unique to his day, but the manner in which he delivered his message is not. Jonah went into a pagan culture, where people had little or no previous knowledge of biblical truth, and he gained a hearing from a scripturally illiterate people, something many today seem to think cannot happen. The fruit of Jonah's ministry was unparalleled, as he saw the greatest positive response recorded anywhere in the Bible. Without entertainment or amusement and without a marketing scheme or an advertising campaign, Jonah simply preached. God's strategy for reaching this entire culture was for His servant to preach.

The book of Jonah is the remarkable account of *one* man (Jonah), equipped with *one* message (God's), committed to *one* method (preaching), who effected great spiritual change. It is no different today. God's work must be done God's way if it is to know God's blessing.

THE CALL TO BIBLICAL PREACHING

First, the power of biblical preaching is rooted and grounded in God's sovereign calling of His chosen servant. This heavenly summons is foundational to powerful preaching. Those whom God calls to preach His Word must know they are divinely selected to carry out His assignment. Jonah was one such man. God spoke "to Jonah the second time, saying, 'Arise, go to Nineveh the great city and proclaim to it the proclamation which I am going to tell you'" (Jon. 3:1–2).

A SPECIFIC PERSON

This scene begins with the call of God extended to a specific person—Jonah. Previously the prophet had resisted God's call to preach in Nineveh (1:3), but graciously God reissued His call. In a sense Jonah was now back where he had begun.[2] This recommissioning of Jonah points to God's own commitment to carry out His will, even working in spite of His servants' failures.

God's summons to preach has always been issued to sovereignly selected individuals, never vaguely to the masses. From all Israel, God chose Moses to be His mouthpiece (Exod. 3:1–8). Similarly the Lord told Jeremiah that before he was born he had been divinely set apart to proclaim His word (Jer. 1:5). While John the Baptist was still in his mother's womb, God appointed him to be His spokesman (Luke 1:15–17). The Lord Jesus personally chose the twelve disciples to be sent out to preach (Mark 3:13–14). The apostle Paul was also chosen by God "from my mother's womb" to herald the unsearchable riches of Christ (Gal. 1:15–16).

The same is true today. God Himself still summons His chosen instruments to the task of preaching, and He then empowers them to do so. Each person who preaches God's message must know that he has been sovereignly called by Christ to represent Him in this solemn duty. In fact, the deep conviction of one's own calling to the ministry is a strong pillar of support during times of adversity. The call to preach should help strengthen all whom God has selected for His service.

A SPECIFIC PLACE

Jonah was commissioned by God to preach in a specific place—Nineveh. Situated on the Tigris River, this city served as the capital of the mighty Assyrians.[3] Three times Nineveh is described as a "great city" (1:2; 3:2; 4:11) and once as "an exceedingly great city" (3:3). This bulging metropolis boasted a population of at least 120,000 (4:11). By way of comparison, Samaria, the capital city of Israel's northern kingdom, had a population of only about thirty thousand, and Jerusalem, capital of the southern kingdom, was even smaller. This great city, Nineveh, was protected by a huge inner wall that was fifty feet wide, one hundred feet high, and about eight miles in circumference. A second line of defense, an outer wall, encompassed fields and the smaller suburban towns.[4]

One of the most wicked cities of the ancient world, Nineveh was feared for the cruelty with which its soldiers treated captives of neighboring nations. The Ninevites were infamous for sacrificing their own children to pagan deities and were shameless in their disregard for human life. No wonder it was known as "the bloody city" (Nah. 3:1). Today modern archaeology has documented the vile brutality of the Assyrians as a barbaric people, especially in their treatment of prisoners of war.[5] This defiant city was not an easy place in which to serve God. Ministering in this "great city" was a most demanding assignment for Jonah.

Lest there be any misunderstanding, there are no easy places today to which God sends His servants to preach. Like Jonah, every ministry assignment is difficult and demanding. Because sin has permeated the entire human race, wherever there are people there will be human depravity. Furthermore, Satan holds all unbelievers captive to his will (2 Tim. 2:25–26). "The whole world lies in the power of the evil one" (1 John 5:19). The world, the flesh, and the devil oppose ministers in every place with sinister, superhuman powers, hostile to the proclamation of the gospel. Wherever God's servants are sent, a battlefield of spiritual warfare awaits them.

A SPECIFIC PURPOSE

Furthermore, God also called Jonah to a specific purpose —preaching. God said that he was to "proclaim . . . the proclamation which I am going to tell you" (3:2). This included both the manner ("proclaim") and the message ("the proclamation"). God would tell him what to say and also how to say it. The Hebrew word for "proclaim," (קְרָא) means to "call, invoke, summon, proclaim, or appeal to," according to the *New International Dictionary of Old Testament Theology and Exegesis*. This often refers to a proclamation spoken in a time of critical need, intended to elicit a decisive response (Pss. 34:6; 81:7).[6] "In prophetic literature the verb קְרָ is a technical term for the proclamation of Yahweh's will."[7] Far more than making mere suggestions or offering idle opinions, this word means to declare a prophetic message (1 Kings 13:32) in the sense of an authoritative proclamation (Gen. 41:43; Exod. 32:5; Judg. 21:13; Esth. 6:9). So Jonah's message was to be given with divine authority.

Concerning the message itself, God referred to it as "the proclamation which I am going to tell you" (Jon. 3:2). In other words, the message originated with God Himself, not the prophet. The word "proclamation" (קְרִיאָה) suggests a formal type of announcement made by an official messenger or ambassador, which lent credence to the importance of the message.[8] Hugh Martin, esteemed eighteenth-century minister of the Free Church of Scotland, wrote, "He is to be an ambassador in the strictest possible sense. He has simply to make known the will and Word of God."[9] In other words, Jonah was to be faithful to deliver God's message, not his own self-contrived thoughts.

In response to God's call of Jonah, this time he obeyed. He was now resolved to proclaim God's message. "So Jonah arose and went to Nineveh according to the word of the Lord. Now Nineveh was an exceedingly great city, a three days' walk" (v. 3). Jonah may have been standing somewhere near the shore of the Mediterranean Sea, having been recently vomited up there by the great fish (2:10). More than five hundred miles away lay the city of Nineveh, and so Jonah's journey there would have taken about a month to complete.[10] The previous time God called him, Jonah headed west; but this time he headed northeast. The city was so vast, it required "a three days' walk" to traverse its circumference of about sixty miles. Nevertheless, such an imposing city did not stifle Jonah's commitment to preach. No longer running from God, he now purposed to go where God wanted him to go and to do what God wanted him to do.

GOD'S PRIMARY PLAN TODAY

Preaching was God's strategy to reach Nineveh, and it remains His primary plan for impacting cities today. With a holy boldness to preach His Word, preachers in this present hour must be obedient to go where they are sent to herald God's saving message. Such a supreme obedience to the Lord by His preachers is *always* necessary. One God-called man armed with one God-sent message, committed to one God-prescribed method—preaching—is *always* sufficient for *any* situation.

John Knox was one such man. Though he would become the leader of the Protestant Reformation in Scotland, Knox entered the ministry only reluctantly. The magnitude of the responsibility to preach the Word was too great for Knox to assume it lightly. For this reformer-in-the-making, the pulpit was a *sacred* desk, a stepping onto *holy* ground. When Knox was extended the pastoral call by his first congregation in April 1547, he immediately burst into tears and withdrew into seclusion, too overwhelmed to accept this call. Knox was all too aware of the divine accountability that accompanied such a calling, to say nothing of his own inadequacies. But God was calling. That undeniable reality arrested his soul.

It was through such a soul-searching experience that Knox knew he *must* preach. Where, it must be asked, are such trembling men today? Where are those who so preach as if by divine appointment? Are *you* this kind of man?

THE CHARACTER OF BIBLICAL PREACHING

The first day Jonah set foot in Nineveh he began preaching. "Then Jonah began to go through the city one day's walk." His message was simple: "Yet forty days and Nineveh will be overthrow" (3:4).

This message is only eight words in the New American Standard Bible; in Hebrew, it has only five words. Although it is not clear that this was all Jonah said, the verse does suggest that God's message was brief. It was a declaration of God's impending judgment, as well as an invitation to His saving grace. From this pointed message, several marks of biblical preaching can be identified.

COURAGEOUS PREACHING

First, Jonah's preaching was courageous. In delivering this message, Jonah "cried out" (v. 4), showing the courage of his soul to declare God's message. He did not creep into town quietly, nor move among the people timidly, only to mumble his message for fear of offending someone. Rather, the prophet raised his voice above the commotion of this great city and proclaimed God's Word. He *had* to be heard.

Jonah did not passively bring up the subject of divine

judgment as if anticipating that his message would be disliked. Instead, he threatened his listeners with divine wrath and eternal destruction. Jonah might have rationalized, *I could be killed if I preach this message. What good would I be to God if I were dead?* Or, *What if the first person to hear me should stone me? How can I reach this city then?* But he did not do this. Instead he courageously spoke out the Lord's message to this citadel of carnality. With a growing boldness in God, who called him to preach, Jonah lifted up his voice for everyone to hear.

The courageous courier of God's Word seems to be an antiquated reminder of a bygone era. Addressing this dire need for boldness in preaching, John Stott wrote:

> *There is an urgent need for courageous preachers in the pulpits of the world today, like the apostles in the early Church who "were filled with the Holy Spirit and spoke the Word of God with boldness" (Acts 4:31, cf. v. 13). Neither men-pleasers nor time-servers ever make good preachers. We are called to the sacred task of biblical exposition, and commissioned to proclaim what God has said, not what human beings want to hear. Many modern churchmen suffer from a malady called "itching ears," which induces them to accumulate for themselves teachers to suit their own likings (2 Timothy 4:3). But we have no liberty to scratch their itch or pander to their likings.*[11]

Unfortunately, much of contemporary preaching seems out of balance, having become too much like what someone described as "a mild-mannered man standing before mild-mannered people urging them to be more mild-mannered." What Philips Brooks said in his famous 1877 Yale Lectures on Preaching sounds a much-needed warning:

> *If you are afraid of men and a slave to their opinion, go and do something else. Go and make shoes to fit them. Go even and paint*

*pictures which you know are bad, but which suit their bad taste.
But do not keep on all your life preaching sermons which say not
what God sent you to declare, but what they have you to say. Be
courageous.*[12]

COMPELLING PREACHING

Second, Jonah's preaching was compelling. The fact that
Jonah "cried out" reveals the passion with which he delivered God's message. This is the same Hebrew word (קְרָא)
that God used earlier in His call on the prophet's life (1:1).
He was dealing with sobering issues of life and death, salvation and damnation, heaven and hell. Alexander Maclaren,
Scottish preacher of the nineteenth century, commented on
the manner of Jonah's preaching:

*To cry . . . suggests the manner befitting those who bear God's
message. They should sound it out loudly, plainly, urgently with
earnestness and marks of emotion in their voices. Languid whis-
pers will not wake up sleepers. Unless the messenger is manifestly
in earnest, the message will fall flat. Not with bated breath as if
ashamed of it, nor with hesitation as if not quite sure of it, nor
with coldness as if it were of little urgency—is God's Word to be
pealed in men's ears. The preacher is a crier.*[13]

God's messengers have always recognized this indispensable need for passion in preaching. Puritan pastor
Richard Baxter said, "I preach as never sure to preach again,
and as a dying man to dying men." George Whitefield commented, "I love those that thunder out the Word. The Christian world is in a deep sleep. Nothing but a loud voice can
awaken them out of it." D. L. Moody remarked, "The best
way to revive a church is to build a fire in the pulpit." Martyn Lloyd-Jones, the late pastor of London's Westminster

Chapel, once said, "Preaching is theology coming through a man who is on fire."[14]

But, to the contrary, levity and even triviality seem to be the order of the day in preaching. Many pastors seem to be more intent on being entertainers than being expositors. Pastor Alistair Begg diagnosed this ailment pointedly when he wrote, "Pulpits are for preachers. We build stages for performers."[15] Issuing a call for gravity in the pulpit, John Piper wrote:

> *Laughter seems to have replaced repentance as the goal of many preachers. Laughter means people feel good. It means they like you, it means you have moved them. It means you have some measure of power. It seems to have all the marks of successful communication—if the depth of sin and the holiness of God and the danger of hell and need for broken hearts is left out of account.*[16]

Sad to say, there is very little compelling, weighty proclamation in our pulpits today. An endless supply of horizontal sharing, frivolous talking, mindless entertaining, and shallow storytelling abounds, but precious little *declaring* the divine message. Nevertheless, the call to preach is a call to do just that—*preach!* There must be a prophetic tone in bringing God's message. Not nervously stuttering as if unsure, nor glibly conversing as if giddy, preaching is to be the profound proclamation of the eternal message which comes from God Himself. If such *gravitas* would be felt by pastors today, like a heavy mantle placed upon their shoulders, the church would see what Jonah saw, namely, greater numbers of sinners converted and saints edified.

CONFRONTATIONAL PREACHING

Third, Jonah's preaching was confrontational. His message —"Yet forty days and Nineveh will be overthrown"—was a declaration of God's impending judgment. This word for "overthrown" (הָפַךְ) is often used of catastrophic judgment.[17] Just as God "overthrew" (הָפַךְ) Sodom and Gomorrah (Gen. 19:25, 29), so He would overthrow Nineveh if the Ninevites did not repent. Jonah was confronting the Ninevites with the severity of God's much-deserved judgment.

Such confrontational preaching was not unique to Jonah. From Moses to Malachi, this same strident tone reverberated in the voices of all the prophets as they issued their calls for stubborn Israel to repent. The preaching of John the Baptist and the Lord Jesus was confrontational, often calling the religious establishment of their day into account (Luke 3:1–17). The apostles reproved those who heard them, going so far as to indict their Jewish listeners for the premeditated murder of the Messiah (Acts 2:23; 4:10; 5:30). The apostle Paul charged Timothy and Titus to proclaim God's Word with elements of reproof, correction, rebuke, and conviction (2 Tim. 3:16; 4:2–4; Titus 1:9; 2:15). And the ascended Jesus confronted five of the seven churches in Asia Minor with their sin as He called them to repent (Revelation 2–3).

Such direct preaching has always marked the proclamation of God's men down through the ages. Someone has quipped:

> *Noah's message from the steps going up to the Ark was not "Something good is going to happen to you!" Amos was not confronted by the high priest of Israel for proclaiming, "Confession is possession!" Jeremiah was not put into the pit for preaching, "I'm O.K., you're O.K." Daniel was not put into the lion's den for telling people, "Possibility thinking will move mountains!" John the Baptist was not forced to preach in the wilderness and eventually beheaded because he preached, "Smile, God loves you!" The two prophets of the tribulation will not be killed for preaching, "God is in his heaven and all is right with the world!"*[18]

Pastors who are committed to biblical exposition must have a confrontive element in their preaching if they are to emulate the prophets and the apostles. Regrettably, this kind of reproof and rebuke is often missing from present-day preaching. Pastor Adrian Rogers calls for boldness in proclaiming God's truth by stating,

> *It is better to be divided by truth than to be united in error. It is better to speak the truth that hurts and then heals, than falsehood that comforts and then kills. It is not love and it is not friendship if we fail to declare the whole counsel of God. It is better to be hated for telling truth than to be loved for telling a lie. . . . It's better to stand alone with the truth than to be wrong with a multitude.*[19]

COMPASSIONATE PREACHING

Fourth, Jonah's preaching was marked by the offer of God's grace and mercy, as he held forth a brief window of time—forty days—in which the Ninevites could repent. As John Hannah noted, "Perhaps this was a period of grace, giving the people an opportunity to repent before the judgment fell!"[20] "Jonah's message," Bible scholar Douglas Stuart wrote, "must have seemed to many Ninevites to be an invitation to repentance, giving hope that they and their city or land might not be destroyed."[21] God extended to the Ninevites a gracious opportunity for them to turn to the Lord and escape the retribution they deserved.

Jonah understood that his message was a loving offer of salvation, for later he said to God, "Thou art a gracious and compassionate God, slow to anger and abundant in lovingkindness, and one who relents concerning calamity" (Jon. 4:2). According to God's abundant grace toward sinners, Nineveh had forty days to repent before His judgment would fall.

Such loving compassion must always accompany biblical preaching. As preachers warn of God's coming judgment, divine grace and tender mercy must be held forth as well. God delights in bestowing pardon on undeserving sinners so that He can reveal His loving-kindness. He says, "I take no pleasure in the death of the wicked" (Ezek. 33:11; cf. 18:23). Finding no joy in the damnation of the unrighteous, He prefers to forgive. He declared Himself to be "compassionate and gracious, slow to anger, and abounding in lovingkindness and truth; who keeps lovingkindness for thousands, who forgives iniquity, transgression and sin" (Exod. 34:6–7). Biblical preaching must accurately convey this aspect of God's loving character. The declaration of God's judgment must be tempered with promises of His mercy; the announcement of His condemnation must be balanced with affirmations of His compassion.

To be sure, the missing power of present-day preaching will be recaptured only when the proclamation of the Word is again courageous, compelling, confrontive, and compassionate, as it was in Jonah's ministry.

THE CONSEQUENCES OF BIBLICAL PREACHING

As the prophet preached God's message, the people of Nineveh listened and responded. Nineveh experienced an unprecedented time of divine visitation as God's message, ministered by the power of God's Spirit, impacted this city. What resulted was a great awakening, a spontaneous stirring in the hearts of those who were under the impending judgment of God.

The word "revival" is used in the following pages to describe the Ninevites' response, but in reality it was a spiritual awakening in which sinners were aroused from their perilous condition of separation from God. In response, they turned to God in repentance and faith. Here was a revival that was saving, sobering, sweeping, and sanctifying.

A SAVING REVIVAL

"Then the people of Nineveh believed in God" (3:5). In response to the preaching of God's message, this "bloody" city, known for its violence, turned to God, entrusting themselves to Him. They turned from their pagan religion of manmade idols and put their trust in the one true God. Some scholars find such a wholesale turning to God unlikely, because Assyrian records make no mention of this citywide revival. But, it was the practice of official ancient historians to delete events that were embarrassing to their cause.[22] For example, Egyptian records made no mention of the Israelites crossing the Red Sea and the drowning of Egypt's army (Exodus 14). Neither did the Assyrians record the killing of 185,000 of their soldiers in Jerusalem (2 Kings 19:35). Yet both events did occur.

So this spiritual awakening should not be discounted simply because secular history did not record it. Furthermore, Jesus Himself validated the genuineness of the Ninevites' conversion. "The men of Nineveh will stand up with this generation at the judgment and condemn it, because they repented at the preaching of Jonah" (Luke 11:32). Also, God would not have removed His hand of judgment against the Ninevites if their response had been superficial.[23] It seems that the people of this ungodly city did truly believe and so received eternal life.[24]

The word "believe" (אָמַן) means "to be firm, to stand firm, to trust, to believe," specifically to "believe in" (Exod. 4:31; Ps. 116:10).[25] It is used of Abram's trust in the Lord. "And [Abram] believed in the Lord; and He reckoned it to him as righteousness" (Gen. 15:6). This does not imply that Abram merely gave intellectual assent to what God said. Instead, he believed God with an active, confident faith, resulting in his salvation (Rom. 4:1–5). In other words, Abram entered into a personal relationship with God Himself by faith.[26] So it is reasonable to infer that when the people of Nineveh heard Jonah's message, they placed their faith in the true God.[27] "They took Jonah's message seriously as a message which actually came from God."[28]

If churches today are to see more people come to Christ, then *more* biblical preaching is needed, not less. God has promised to honor His Word. "Faith comes from hearing, and hearing by the word of Christ" (Rom. 10:17). God has always been pleased to use the foolishness of preaching His Word to bring about the conversion of lost sinners (1 Cor. 1:18–25). He did so in Jonah's day, and He will do so now *if* churches will return to solid, straightforward biblical preaching.

A SOBERING REVIVAL

The faith of the Ninevites was accompanied by expressions of deep sorrow and humble contrition over their sin. Having been deeply affected by Jonah's message, they demonstrated that their repentance was genuine as "they called a fast and put on sackcloth" (Jon. 3:5). In the ancient world, a "fast" was often a sign of inward contrition and self-humiliation (1 Sam. 7:6; 2 Sam. 1:12; Neh. 1:4; Zech. 7:5), and wearing "sackcloth" was also an outward symbol of an inward sorrow over sin. Sackcloth was a coarse, roughly woven, burlap-like fabric, often made of goat's hair. It was rough, dark, crude, and uncomfortable to wear. It was the normal dress of poor people, prisoners, and slaves, and was often worn by people when they were in mourning (Ezek. 7:18). Prophets wore it (2 Kings 1:8; Zech. 13:4; Mark 1:6), partly to associate with the poor and at other times as a sign of mourning for the sins of the people.[29] The abrasiveness of the sackcloth made the one who wore it miserable from the self-inflicted pain, which was intentionally symbolic. It represented how the Ninevites felt internally about the painful awareness of their sin. They were sorrowful, miserable, broken, and grief-stricken over their sin as they suddenly realized that their wickedness had offended God. Understanding their inability to contend with God, they chose to be in submission to Him as the supreme Ruler of heaven and earth.

A similar experience of repentance is desperately needed today. Although not necessarily expressed by donning sackcloth, genuine repentance involves a deep conviction of sin, a sorrow over sin, and turning from sin. Such a sobering revival will be seen again only when preaching once more calls sinners to repent and turn from their wicked ways.

A SWEEPING REVIVAL

Every stratum of society in Nineveh repented—"from the greatest to the least of them" (Jon. 3:5). From princes to paupers, from royalty to rogues, they were all broken over their sins and turned to God. This response was citywide in its scope, blanketing the entire community.[30] In fact, so sweeping was this revival that even the king's heart was smitten. "When the word reached the king of Nineveh, he arose from his throne, laid aside his robe from him, covered himself with sackcloth, and sat on the ashes" (v. 6).

When the king of Nineveh heard God's message, he became deeply convicted and wounded, as evidenced by his change of outward clothing. Descending from his throne, he exchanged his silk robes for sackcloth and sat down on ashes, yet another sign of deep humiliation (cf. Job 42:6; Isa. 58:5). With no attempt to cover up his sin, he openly acknowledged his iniquity before God.

So genuine was this work of God in the king's heart that he issued a decree for the entire city of Nineveh to go one step further in expressing its repentance. "And he issued a proclamation and it said, 'In Nineveh by the decree of the king and his nobles: Do not let man, beast, herd, or flock taste a thing. Do not let them eat or drink water. But both man and beast must be covered with sackcloth'" (3:7–8).

The king's edict called for an all-encompassing fast that was to include the animals as well. Including domestic animals in mourning ceremonies was a common way in which people expressed deep remorse and supplication.[31] So by official statement even the animals were to be covered with sackcloth to depict the thorough repentance of the entire populace. After winning over his cabinet and advisers, the king called on the entire nation to join him in this intense period of penitence.

So it is today. When sparked by the preaching of God's Word, a true work of His Spirit knows no social boundaries. Not restricted to a particular economic class, ethnic group, or religious denomination, a heaven-sent spiritual awakening extends from top to bottom, touching all classes of people. Not limited to one particular homogeneous unit, it transcends all cultural differences and social barriers. Only the preaching of God's Word can bring about such a thorough, across-the-board response.

A SANCTIFIYING REVIVAL

This previously pagan king, now converted, invited all his subjects to join him in turning from the violent deeds that previously characterized their lives. The decree he issued said, "And let men call on God earnestly that each may turn from his wicked way and from the violence which is in his hands" (v. 8). In this royal edict, repentance and faith were inseparably joined, like the head and tail of the same coin. In calling each citizen to turn from his "wicked way and from the violence which is in his hands," he evoked a tandem expression, which is a typical way of joining the general with the specific.[32] The word for "wicked way" (רָעָה) refers to sin broadly and generically, everything condemned by divine law and human conscience.[33] But "violence" (חָמָס) represents the infringement of human rights or a defiance of common decency (cf. Gen. 16:5). It suggests moral misbehavior and aggressive violence toward other peoples and nations, including even murder.[34] Ellison notes, "The Assyrian assumed that in virtue of his conquests he had been placed above lesser breeds and was entitled to ignore the dictates of conscience and compassion in his behavior to his neighbors."[35] But in true repentance the Assyrians renounced their sin.

The Hebrew word for "turn" (שׁוּב) has a variety of meanings, depending on its context. The verb basically means to make a change of direction. In a religious sense, this word is the most common term for turning decisively to either God (or idols), or turning away from Him (or them).[36] "Better than any other verb, it combines in itself the two requirements of repentance: to turn from evil and to turn to the good."[37] The people of Nineveh demonstrated both sides of this turning in repentance by expressing their belief in God (Jon. 3:5) and turning from their wicked ways (v. 8).

The words of the Assyrian king concluded with a contrite expression of hope that God would find their repentance genuine. "Who knows, God may turn and relent, and withdraw His burning anger so that we shall not perish" (v. 9).

The Ninevites truly repented, as evidenced by the way the Lord responded. "When God saw their deeds, that they turned from their wicked ways, then God relented concerning the calamity which He had declared He would bring upon them. And He did not do it" (v. 10). When the Lord saw that their turning to Him was genuine, He withheld His judgment. He was not changing His plan; instead He was responding to their repentance.[38] This is consistent with God's character, for as Jonah said later, He is "gracious and compassionate . . . and one who relents concerning calamity" (4:2). He withheld His judgment, knowing all along what the Ninevites' response would be.[39]

This can be the response to the powerful preaching of God's Word in this hour. The Scripture has *not* lost its power to convert and change the human heart. Where are such men today who will preach the Word as did Jonah?

COURAGEOUS, COMPELLING PREACHING

Evangelical churches need to recapture the power of biblical preaching—preaching that is courageous, compelling, confrontive, and compassionate, as exemplified by Jonah. When Charles Haddon Spurgeon witnessed the decline of dynamic preaching in his day, he pleaded for the Lord to raise up a new generation of biblical preachers.

> *We want again Luthers, Calvins, Bunyans, Whitefields, men fit to mark eras, whose names breathe terror in our foemen's ears. We have dire need of such. Whence will they come to us? They are the gifts of Jesus Christ to the Church, and will come in due time. He has power to give us back again a golden age of preachers, and when the good old truth is once more preached by men whose lips are touched as with a live coal from off the altar, this shall be the instrument in the hand of the Spirit for bringing about a great and thorough revival of religion in the land.*
>
> *I do not look for any other means of converting men beyond the simple preaching of the gospel and the opening of men's ears to hear it. The moment the Church of God shall despise the pulpit, God will despise her. It has been through the ministry that the Lord has always been pleased to revive and bless His Churches.*[40]

May God raise up such proclaimers of His divine truth who will preach with growing confidence in the power of His Word to perform its sacred work. May Christ give to His

church again an army of biblical expositors who will proclaim the Scriptures boldly in the power of the Holy Spirit.

Notes

1. For further reading on the anemic condition of preaching in the evangelical church, see Mark Dever, *Nine Marks of a Healthy Church* (Wheaton, Ill.: Crossway, 2000), 21–42; John H. Armstrong, ed., *The Compromised Church* (Wheaton, Ill.: Crossway, 1998); and Alistair Begg, *Preaching for God's Glory* (Wheaton, Ill.: Crossway, 1999).

2. Billy K. Smith and Frank S. Page, *Amos, Obadiah, Jonah,* New American Commentary (Nashville: Broadman & Holman, 1995), 257.

3. Merrill Unger, *Unger's Commentary on the Old Testament* (Chicago: Moody, 1981), 2:1836.

4. John D. Hannah, "Jonah," in *The Bible Knowledge Commentary, Old Testament,* ed. John F. Walvoord and Roy B. Zuck (Wheaton, Ill.: Victor, 1995), 1468.

5. Unger, *Unger's Commentary on the Old Testament,* 2:1838.

6. Leonard J. Coppes, "קָרָא" in *Theological Wordbook of the Old Testament,* ed. R. Laird Harris, Gleason L. Archer, Jr., Bruce K. Waltke (Chicago: Moody, 1980), 2:810.

7. Louis Jonker, "קרא" in *New International Dictionary of Old Testament Theology and Exegesis,* ed. Willem A. VanGemeren (Grand Rapids: Zondervan, 1997), 3:971.

8. Smith and Page, *Amos, Obadiah, Jonah,* 258.

9. Hugh Martin, *The Prophet Jonah* (London: Banner of Truth, 1978), 253.

10. Smith and Page, *Amos, Obadiah, Jonah,* 259.

11. John R. W. Stott, *Between Two Worlds* (Grand Rapids: Eerdmans, 1982), 299.

12. Philips Brooks, *Lectures on Preaching* (New York: Dutton, 1877), 59.

13. Alexander Maclaren, *Expositions of Holy Scripture* (Grand Rapids: Baker, 1994) 6:190–91.

14. Richard Baxter as quoted in John Blanchard, comp., *Gathered Gold* (Darlington, Del.: Evangelical Press, 1984), 236; George Whitefield as quoted in Blanchard, 237; D. L. Moody as quoted in Blanchard, 236; and Martyn Lloyd-Jones as quoted in Blanchard, 236.

15. Alistair Begg, *Preaching for God's Glory* (Wheaton: Crossway, 1999), 11.

16. John Piper, *The Supremacy of God in Preaching* (Grand Rapids: Baker, 1990), 5–56.

17. K. Seybold, "הפך" in *Theological Dictionary of the Old Testament,* ed. G. Johannes Botterweck and Helmer Ringgren (Grand Rapids: Eerdmans, 1997), 3:424. This Hebrew root, together with its derivatives, appears more than one hundred times in the Old Testament and is primarily found in association with the expression of God's awesome anger and fierce wrath unleashed on the unrepentant, such as Sodom and Gomorrah (Gen. 19:21, 25, 29;

Deut. 29:23; Isa. 13:19; Jer. 20:16, 49:18; 50:40; Lam. 4:6; Amos 4:11). It was used to describe God's overturning the wicked through judgment.

18. Michael Green, ed., *Illustrations for Biblical Preaching* (Grand Rapids: Baker, 1997), 301 (italics added).

19. Adrian Rogers, "The Triumph of Truth," *Berean Call,* December 1996, 3.

20. Hannah, "Jonah," 1469.

21. Douglas Stuart, *Hosea-Jonah,* Word Biblical Commentary (Waco: Word, 1987), 489.

22. Hannah, "Jonah," 1469.

23. Smith and Page, *Amos, Obadiah, Jonah,* 265.

24. Patrick Fairbairn, *Jonah: His Life, Character, and Mission* (Grand Rapids: Baker, 1980), 123.

25. William L. Holladay, ed., *A Concise Hebrew and Aramaic Lexicon of the Old Testament* (Grand Rapids: Eerdmans, 1988), 20.

26. The verbal form found in Jonah not only implies the acceptance of what someone says is true, but it also "has the added sense of acting in response to what is heard with trust or obedience," according to R. W. L. Moberly, "אמן" in *New International Dictionary of Old Testament Theology and Exegesis,* 1:431.

27. Wayne G. Strickland, "Isaiah, Jonah, and Religious Pluralism," *Bibliotheca Sacra* 153 (January–March 1996): 32.

28. Alfred Jepsen, "אמן" in *Theological Dictionary of the Old Testament,* 1:305.

29. Smith and Page, *Amos, Obadiah, Jonah,* 266.

30. Stuart, *Hosea-Jonah,* 489.

31. Unger, *Unger's Commentary on the Old Testament,* 2:1837–38.

32. Smith and Page, *Amos, Obadiah, Jonah,* 270.

33. G. Herbert Livingston, "רָעָה" in *Theological Wordbook of the Old Testament,* 2:856.

34. R. Laird Harris, "חָמָס" in *Theological Wordbook of the Old Testament,* 1:297.

35. H. L. Ellison, "Jonah," in *The Expositor's Bible Commentary* (Grand Rapids: Zondervan, 1985), 7:383.

36. John N. Oswalt, "שׁוּב" in *New International Dictionary of Old Testament Theology and Exegesis,* 3:56–57.

37. Victor P. Hamilton, "שׁוּב" in *Theological Wordbook of the Old Testament,* 2:909.

38. Marvin R. Wilson, "נָחַם" in *Theological Wordbook of the Old Testament,* 2:571.

39. For discussions on God's omniscience and immutability see Bruce A. Ware, *God's Lesser Glory* (Wheaton, Ill.: Crossway, 2000); Norman Geisler, *Creating God in the Image of Man?* (Minneapolis: Bethany, 1982); Thomas R. Schreiner and Bruce A. Ware, *Still Sovereign* (Grand Rapids: Baker, 2000); and Michael S. Horton, *A Confessing Theology for Postmodern Times* (Wheaton, Ill.: Crossway, 2000).

40. Charles Haddon Spurgeon, *The Early Years, C. H. Spurgeon Autobiography,* vol. 1 (London: Banner of Truth, 1962), v.

F or Ezra had set his heart to study the law of the Lord, and to practice it, and to teach His statutes and ordinances in Israel. And all the people gathered as one man at the square which was in front of the Water Gate, and they asked Ezra the scribe to bring the book of the law of Moses which the Lord had given to Israel. Then Ezra the priest brought the law before the assembly of men, women, and all who could listen with understanding, on the first day of the seventh month. And he read from it before the square which was in front of the Water Gate from early morning until midday, in the presence of men and women, those who could understand; and all the people were attentive to the book of the law. And Ezra the scribe stood at a wooden podium which they had made for the purpose. . . . And Ezra opened the book in the sight of all the people . . .; and when he opened it, all the people stood up. Then Ezra blessed the Lord the great God. And all the people answered, "Amen, Amen!" while lifting up their hands; then they bowed low and worshiped the Lord with their faces to the ground. Also Jeshua, Bani, Sherebiah, Jamin, Akkub, Shabbethai, Hodiah, Maaseiah, Kelita, Azariah, Jozabad, Hanan, Pelaiah, and the Levites, explained the law to the people while the people remained in their place. And they read from the book, from the law of God, translating to give the sense so that they understood the reading.

Then Nehemiah, who was the governor, and Ezra the priest and scribe, and the Levites who taught the people said to all the people, "This day is holy to the Lord your God; do not mourn or weep." For all the people were weeping when they heard the words of the law. Then he said to them, "Go, eat of the fat, drink of the sweet, and send portions to him who has nothing prepared; for this day is holy to our Lord. Do not be grieved, for the joy of the Lord is your strength." So the Levites calmed all the people, saying, "Be still, for the day is holy; do not be grieved." And all the people went away to eat, to drink, to send portions and to celebrate a great festival, because they understood the words which had been made known to them.

Then on the second day the heads of fathers' households of all the people, the priests, and the Levites were gathered to Ezra the scribe that they might gain insight into the words of the law. And they found written in the law how the Lord had commanded through Moses that the sons of Israel should live in booths during the feast of the seventh month. So they proclaimed and circulated a proclamation in all their cities and in Jerusalem, saying, "Go out to the hills, and bring olive branches, and wild olive branches, myrtle branches, palm branches, and branches of other leafy trees, to make booths, as it is written." So the people went out and brought them and made booths for themselves, each on his roof, and in their courts, and in the courts of the house of God, and in the square at the Water Gate, and in the square at the Gate of Ephraim. And the entire assembly of those who had returned from the captivity made booths and lived in them. The sons of Israel had indeed not done so from the days of Joshua the son of Nun to that day. And there was great rejoicing. And he read from the book of the law of God daily, from the first day to the last day. And they celebrated the feast seven days, and on the eighth day there was a solemn assembly according to the ordinance.

EZRA 7:10; NEHEMIAH 8:1–18

*"A holy minister is
an awful weapon in the hand of God."*

❖ Robert Murray McCheyne

3

BRING THE BOOK!
THE PATTERN OF BIBLICAL PREACHING

WALTER KAISER, a leading evangelical scholar, issued a simple but striking statement in his commencement address at Dallas Theological Seminary in April 2000—a stirring challenge that should grip the hearts of all who are called to the ministry of biblical preaching and teaching. Those who enter the pulpit to preach, Kaiser admonished, should always be pointing to a text of Scripture.

When a man preaches, he should never remove his finger from the Scriptures, Kaiser charged. If he is gesturing with his right hand, he should keep his left hand's finger on the text. If he reverses hands for gesturing, then he should also reverse hands for holding his spot in the text. He should *always* be pointing to the Scriptures.[1]

This is sound advice. Both literally and figuratively, the preacher should always be pointing to a biblical text. This Word-centered focus in the pulpit is the defining mark of all true expositors. Those who preach and teach the Word are to be so deeply rooted and grounded in the Scriptures that they never depart from them, ever directing themselves as well as their listeners to its truths. Biblical preaching should be just that—*biblical*—and all who stand in the pulpit must show an unwavering, even relentless, commitment to the Scripture itself. As a practicing physician knows and prescribes medicine, so every preacher should be ever studying, learning, and dispensing heavy doses of the healing balm of God's Word to all his patients. Whatever the ailment, there is but one cure for the soul—the Word of God applied by the Spirit of God to the human heart.

THE MISSING PRESCRIPTION

But this biblical prescription is an unknown remedy for many preachers today. In their zeal to lead popular and successful ministries, many are becoming less concerned with pointing to the biblical text. Their use of the Bible is much like the singing of the national anthem before a ball game—something merely heard at the beginning, but never referenced again, a necessary preliminary that becomes an awkward intrusion into the real event. In their attempt to be contemporary and relevant, many pastors talk *about* the Scriptures, but, sadly, they rarely speak *from* them. Instead, they rush headlong to the next personal illustration, humorous anecdote, sociological quote, or cultural reference, rarely to return to the biblical text. How can pastors expect dying souls to become spiritually healthy if they never give them the prescribed remedy? How can pastors expect sinners to be converted and Christians to be sanctified if they fail to expound God's Word (1 Pet. 1:23–25; John 17:17)?

Writing almost a half century ago, Merrill Unger saw this dangerous departure from biblical preaching already at hand and threatening the vitality of the church. Sounding a warning, he wrote, "To an alarming extent the glory is departing from the pulpit of the twentieth century. The basic reason for this gloomy condition is obvious. That which imparts the glory has been taken away from the center of so much of our modern preaching and placed on the periphery. The Word of God has been denied the throne and given a subordinate place."[2]

What Unger saw looming on the horizon—the dearth of expository preaching—is now fully upon the church. "Where such exposition and authoritative declaration of the Word of God are abandoned," Unger wrote, "Ichabod, the glory is departed, must be written over the preacher and over the pulpit from which he preaches."[3] At the dawn of the twenty-first century, the renowned expository preacher James Boice reinforced Unger's words. Writing shortly before his death, Boice warned, "These are not good days for the evangelical church, and anyone who takes a moment to evaluate the life and outlook of evangelical churches will understand that."[4]

Now, more than ever, pastors must come back to the centrality of the Word of God and preach it in the power of the Holy Spirit if the church is to be put back on the right course.

A PATTERN FOR ALL PREACHERS

Amid the many examples held before preachers today, one biblical expositor who stands out as worthy of emulation is an Old Testament priest and scribe named Ezra. Once described "as a proficient guardian and expositor of the Mosaic Torah,"[5] this reformer of ancient Israel following the people's return from exile provides a timeless pattern for preachers today.

God used Ezra to ignite a great revival when he returned to Jerusalem (Ezra 7–10). After Zerubbabel led a large contingent of Jews from Babylon to Jerusalem to rebuild the ruined temple (538 B.C.), Ezra escorted a second group to the holy city to restore the Word of God to its rightful place (458 B.C.). As he led God's people to humble themselves beneath the Lord's mighty right hand, the key to Ezra's ministry was undoubtedly his resolute determination to learn, live, and proclaim the Scriptures. The verse that uniquely summarizes his life and ministry is Ezra 7:10, which says that the leader "set his heart to *study* the law of the Lord and to *practice* it, and to *teach* His statutes and ordinances in Israel" (italics added). Here is the threefold pattern of Ezra's ministry. He was thoroughly committed to study, practice, and teach God's Word.

Before opening his mouth to teach the Law, Ezra lived a life of obedience, practicing what he preached. But before he practiced and proclaimed the Word, he first set his heart to study it. God's sovereign hand of blessing was on him (7:6, 28; 8:18, 22, 31) because he was so completely immersed in His Word (7:10). It was Ezra's all-absorbing commitment to the Scriptures that enabled him to impact his generation. These three aspects of his Word-oriented ministry—learn it, live it, and let it out—formed the solid foundation of his life and ministry and provide a clear and compelling pattern for all who preach and teach the Word today. Kidner noted, "He is a model reformer in that what he taught he had first lived, and what he lived he had first made sure of in the Scriptures."[6]

Unquestionably Ezra's life transcends the centuries and challenges this present generation of expositors to a high standard of excellence in the Word, providing "an inviolable order for a successful ministry."[7] All biblical preachers and teachers would do well to follow this pattern of Ezra's ministry, which involved *knowing* ("study"), *being* ("practice"), and *doing* ("proclaiming").

THE PREACHER'S PREPARATION IN THE WORD

First, Ezra was a devoted student of Scripture, seeking to know what the Word said. He was diligent to dig out its rich truths from the inexhaustible mines of God's Word.

"Ezra had set his heart to study the law of the Lord" (7:10). This was the deep shaft in which his spiritual life struck gold—his personal study of the Word. Several marks of his personal study of the Scriptures are worth noting.

CONSUMING STUDY

Ezra's study of God's Word was consuming. The phrase "set his heart" (לְבָבוֹ, הֵכִין) conveys the idea of being firmly committed to a particular course of action with unwavering steadfastness. The verb signifies being "established, prepared, fixed" in a determined pursuit.[8] For example, the same root is used to portray God's intentional acts when He established the heavens (see Prov. 3:19; 8:27). Thus, the expression carries the idea of a determined purpose and unwavering resolution to act in a prescribed way to bring something to pass. The New King James Version renders this, "Ezra had *prepared* his heart to *seek* the law of the Lord" (italics added), underscoring his purposeful activity to pursue the Scriptures intently. Elsewhere, this verb is likewise used to describe fixed intention, settled determination, resolute action (1 Chron. 29:18; 2 Chron. 12:14; Ps. 57:7). This is precisely how Ezra applied himself to the study of the Law. His mind "was zeroed in on the primary intention of studying God's Word."[9] He was not a man of many pursuits in life, but was possessed with one chief concern—the Word of God. "Ezra thus concentrated his whole life on the study of the law."[10]

The "heart," in which Ezra purposed to study the Scriptures, connotes "the totality of man's inner or immaterial nature,"[11] or "the entire inner life of a person."[12] The Hebrew word for "heart" (לֵבָב) represents the center or middle of something, often referring to the physical heart, the blood-pumping organ that supplies life for the entire body. However, of the approximately 850 times it occurs in the Old

Testament, its most common meaning is spiritual, signifying a person's inner or immaterial being—his or her mind, emotions, and will.

Thus, the heart denotes the *intellect,* by which one thinks, analyzes, compares, and understands a matter (1 Kings 3:12; 2 Kings 5:26; 2 Chron. 9:23; Prov. 16:23); the *emotions,* or the deepest innermost feelings of a person (Prov. 17:22, 25:20); and the *volition,* the seat of the will where choices are made (2 Chron. 12:14). When Ezra set "his heart" to study the Word, he poured the whole spectrum of his inner life into doing so. In other words, the study of Scripture absolutely consumed his life.

John Bunyan, seventeenth-century English preacher and author, was also consumed with the study of God's Word. Charles Haddon Spurgeon, who read Bunyan's *Pilgrim's Progress* every year, once remarked about Bunyan, "He had studied our Authorized Version . . . till his whole being was saturated with Scripture; and through his writings . . . he . . . [makes] us feel and say 'Why, this man is living Bible! Prick him anywhere; and you will find that his blood is Bibline; the very essence of the Bible flows from him. He cannot speak without quoting a text, for his soul is full of the Word of God.'"[13] So it must be with all preachers today. The Scripture itself—not merely books *about* the Bible—must saturate the minds of pastors if it is to flow from their lives and lips as "bibline."

CAREFUL STUDY

Further, Ezra was committed to the careful and competent "study" of God's Word. The Hebrew word translated "study" (דָּרַשׁ) in verse 10 means "to seek with care, inquire."[14] For example, this word was used when Moses "searched carefully" to find out what happened to the sin offering (Lev. 10:16) or when David "inquired" to find out who Bathsheba was (2 Sam. 11:3). The word "study" (or "search") includes the idea of "investigating, searching, being concerned about, striving for."[15] As it relates to the investigation of the Scriptures, this word means to "investigate and examine" its true meaning in careful study.[16] Thus, Ezra studied the Word by carefully searching it, investigating its truths, probing its parts, surveying its whole, striving to understand its meaning, being concerned to grasp its message. He was not content to skim the surface and gain a superficial knowledge of the text.

Reflecting on his early days of poring over the Scriptures, Martin Luther said, "When I was young, I read the Bible over and over and over again, and was so perfectly acquainted with it, that I could, in an instant, have pointed to any verse that might have been mentioned."[17] He also wrote, "For a number of years I have now annually read through the Bible twice. If the Bible were a large, mighty tree and all its words were little branches, I have tapped at all the branches, eager to know what was there and what it had to offer."[18]

He once explained why such attention is necessary: "He who is well acquainted with the text of Scripture is a distinguished theologian. For a Bible passage or text is of more value than the comments of four authors."[19] Holding forth Luther's intense, careful study of Scripture as an example for every preacher, John Piper wrote, "At the heart of every pastor's work is bookwork. Call it reading, meditation, reflection, cogitation, study, exegesis, or whatever you will—a large and central part of our work is to wrestle God's meaning from a book, and then to proclaim it in the power of the Holy Spirit."[20] If the preacher is to be powerful in the pulpit, he must first be proficient in his study.

COMPREHENSIVE STUDY

Moreover, Ezra pursued a comprehensive study of God's Word. This is seen in the way he studied "the law of the Lord" and applied its "statutes and ordinances." This comprehensive threefold designation—the Law of the Lord, statutes, and ordinances—indicates that he studied *all* facets of God's Word. Tradition says Ezra was the founder of the Great Synagogue, where the Old Testament canon was first recognized. Another tradition says that Ezra had memorized the entire Law of God.[21] The point is that Ezra pored over the full counsel of God written in holy Scripture, mastering its content, leaving no part unexplored. No wonder he was described as a "skilled" scribe of the Word (Ezra 7:6). As a "skilled" (מָרִיר) person, he was "a professional of highest order,"[22] displaying expert precision with the entire biblical text. Such skill was the result of his diligent study.

"GIVE ME THAT BOOK!"

Every preacher must follow Ezra's example and be committed to the study of the Scriptures in a way that is consuming, careful, and comprehensive. Pastors must guard against the seemingly endless, mounting pressures placed on them to sacrifice their study of the Word on the altar of their growing list of "priorities." A shrinking study time will result in shrinking power in the pulpit. The church needs more men like John Wesley, the powerful eighteenth-century preacher who cried out, "O give me that Book! At any price, give me the book of God."[23] All expositors must be serious students of God's Word, willing to devote themselves to the relentless pursuit of deepening and expanding their knowledge of biblical truth. The day the preacher stops studying God's Word, whether he realizes it or not, is the day he begins losing spiritual passion and vitality in his preaching.

In a revealing interview, Billy Graham was asked, "If you had to live your life over again, what would you do differently?" His answer is noteworthy. "One of my great regrets is that I have not studied enough. I wish I had studied more and preached less. People have pressured me into speaking to groups when I should have been studying and preparing. Donald Grey Barnhouse said that if he knew the Lord was coming in three years, he would spend two of them studying and one preaching."[24] There is no substitute for the man of God being a diligent student of the Word of God!

THE PREACHER'S PERSONALIZATION OF THE WORD

Second, Ezra was committed to practice the Scriptures in his own life. "For Ezra had set his heart to *study* the law of the Lord, and to *practice* it" (Ezra 7:10, italics added). Ezra mastered the Word, and the Word mastered him. His careful study led to a holy life. His personal integrity became the platform from which he carried out his public teaching ministry. What he learned in the Scriptures, he lived. Thus, *after* he studied the Word and *before* he preached it, he was careful to obey it.

PERSONAL OBEDIENCE

The words translated "set his heart" are directed toward all three of Ezra's activities—his study, practice, and teaching.[25] The same determination that marked his personal study also described his personal obedience. The Hebrew word for "practice," (עָשָׂה), carries the idea of expending energy in the pursuit of something (Exod. 23:22; Lev. 19:37; Deut. 6:18),[26] which in Ezra's case was personal obedience. The Hebrew word for "practice" is used to describe God's creative efforts in making the world (Gen. 1:7, 16, 25–26, 31). This word was also used to describe man's industrious efforts, such as Noah's building the ark (6:14), Jacob's constructing a house (33:17), and the tabernacle workers' making the ark of the covenant (Exod. 25:10–11, 13, 17).

Ezra built the Scriptures into his life through personal obedience. Far from merely stockpiling biblical knowledge in his head, much as raw materials would be stored in a warehouse but not used, Ezra labored to practice the truth he learned, putting it into practice. With much personal effort, he crafted a holy life.

Such personal obedience is essential for all who preach. Those who teach the Word will be held to a higher accountability by God, not only to teach it accurately, but also to live it correctly. As James wrote, "Let not many of you become teachers, my brethren, knowing that as such we shall incur a stricter judgment" (James 3:1). The overseer who is "able to teach" must be "above reproach" in every area of his personal life (1 Tim. 3:2–7). Who would select a banker who is personally bankrupt? Neither will people receive a preacher who does not obey his own message. D. L. Moody once said, "God did not give us the Scriptures to increase our knowledge but to change our lives."27 Such personal transformation is always the expositor's goal in preaching, and it must begin in his life. He must *model* the message.

PROMPT OBEDIENCE

Implied in this threefold sequence of activities in Ezra 7:10—study, practice, teach—is Ezra's prompt obedience of Scripture. *After* he studied the Word and *before* he taught it, he obeyed it. In other words, somewhere between his study and his delivery, the Word was put into practice in his personal life. Here lies a logical, unfolding progression of activities. The second activity ("practice") builds on the first ("study"), and the third ("teach") rests on the first two. Thus, in being quick to obey the moral requirements of the Law of the Lord, Ezra serves as a model for preachers. The expositor must not only practice *what* he preaches, but he must also practice *before* he preaches. Puritan Thomas Adams once noted, "True obedience has no lead at its heels."[28] Nowhere should prompt obedience be more clearly seen than in the life of the one who ministers God's Word. Delayed obedience is *no* obedience. As A.W. Tozer wrote, "Theological truth is useless until it is obeyed. The purpose behind all doctrine is to secure moral action."[29] This is to say, Scripture *learned* is useless until it is *lived*. To know and not to do, as an old adage says, is not to know at all.

PASSIONATE OBEDIENCE

Moreover, Ezra obeyed the Word with the same "heart" devotion with which he studied it. Centuries later, a class of scribes arose in Jesus' day who sought to follow the Law, but *not* from the heart. With full heads but empty hearts, these scribes attempted to teach the Word, which prompted Jesus to say, "This people honors Me with their lips, but their heart is far away from Me" (Matt. 15:8). Ezra, however, was a scribe who *wholeheartedly* kept the Word, not with mere external ritual or empty routine, but with a deep internal desire. Describing this kind of passionate obedience, George Mueller, nineteenth-century church leader in Bristol, England, warned that the Word can be studied, but not obeyed, just as water can run through a pipe and not be absorbed.[30] The Word must be internalized by the preacher before it is passed on to others. His heart cannot be into preaching until his heart is into the Word and the Word is into his heart.

PLENARY OBEDIENCE

Ezra not only studied all the Scripture, he also sought to obey all that it taught. As he labored to understand the whole "Law of the Lord," his was a plenary obedience. He was equally determined to obey all its commands, to follow all its precepts, and to heed all its warnings.

Should it be any different for preachers today? Puritan Thomas Brooks wrote, "No man obeys God truly who does not endeavor to obey God fully."[31] The one who brings the Word must bow first before the Word and fully keep it. Selective obedience is *no* obedience. Partial obedience is nothing more than disguised *disobedience*. To be compelling in the pulpit, preachers must be complete in obedience. Thus, Ezra was given to an obedience that was personal, prompt, passionate, and plenary. Biblical expositors today must follow in this pursuit of personal holiness.

THE PREACHER'S PROCLAMATION OF THE WORD

Third, Ezra was diligent to teach others the Word he learned and lived. Biblical teaching seeks to guide people to follow the will of God, not by offering mere human opinions or suggestions, but by bringing "the authoritative declaration of the Word of God."[32] This is the true nature of biblical preaching and teaching. As John Stott suggests, it is "to open the inspired text with such faithfulness and sensitivity that God's voice is heard and His people obey Him."[33]

How did Ezra teach the Word? Insight is given into Ezra's teaching ministry in the Book of Nehemiah, which records the fact that fourteen years later (444 B.C.) Nehemiah led a third group from Babylon to Jerusalem in order to rebuild the broken walls around the city. Nehemiah 8:1–8, which records one of the greatest revivals in Scripture, reveals facts about how Ezra taught the Word.

REVERENCE FOR THE WORD

As Ezra taught the Word, his heart was gripped with

deep-seated reverence for the Scriptures. Nehemiah 8:1 reads, "And all the people gathered as one man at the square which was in front of the Water Gate, and they asked Ezra the scribe to bring the book of the law of Moses which the Lord had given to Israel." A large multitude—a gathering of 42,360 people—assembled at the square in front of the Water Gate, a site near the rebuilt temple, and asked Ezra to bring out "the book of the law of Moses." He stepped forward before the people with the Scriptures in hand (v. 2), mounted a wooden platform (v. 4), and unrolled the scroll (v. 5). With reverential awe, the people instinctively stood to their feet, recognizing its divine authorship and sovereign authority (v. 5). They knew they would be hearing not a mere man speak his own ideas, but they would be hearing the very Word of God.

With the same reverence, Ezra then offered a benediction to God, blessing His holy name, and the crowd responded by raising their hands and saying, "Amen, Amen" (v. 6). This awe-filled affirmation conveyed the intensity of their reverence for God's Word. With solemn humility, they "bowed low and worshiped the Lord with their faces to the ground" (v. 6). Fear gripped their trembling hearts, for God had spoken to them through His Word.

Such reverence for the Scriptures must always be present in the heart of the preacher. Before the people can be expected to have a healthy, holy fear of the Word, the same soul-gripping reality must mark the one who expounds it. Such reverence was the basis of Paul's charge to young Timothy when he wrote, "I solemnly charge you in the presence of God and of Christ Jesus, who is to judge the living and the dead, and by His appearing and His kingdom: preach the Word" (2 Tim. 4:1–2). Could there be any more heart-sobering motivation by which a preacher would approach the Scriptures than this?

Commenting on the reverential awe with which Martin

Luther entered the pulpit, Spurgeon once said, "I believe Luther would have faced the internal fiend himself without a fear; and yet we have his own confession that his knees often knocked together when he stood up to preach. He trembled lest he should not be faithful to God's Word. To preach the whole truth is an awful charge. You and I, who are ambassadors for God, must not trifle, but we must tremble at God's Word."[34] John Calvin noted, "We owe to the Scripture the same reverence which we owe to God because it has proceeded from Him alone, and has nothing of man mixed with it."[35]

But let's face it: Too many preachers today bear more resemblance to entertainers than expositors, stand-up comics rather than knee-shaking servants. God-fearing, awe-struck men in pulpits remain the need of the hour. John Knox, the great Scottish Reformer, once said, "I have never once feared the devil, but I tremble every time I enter the pulpit." Where are such men who, like Knox, tremble when they open the Word of God?

READING THE WORD

Surrounded by certain Levites, Ezra read aloud the text. Nehemiah records, "They read from the book, from the law of God, translating to give the sense so that they understood the reading" (8:8). Before the Word was explained, it was introduced to the minds of the listeners through its public reading. This was no dull, dry reading of the biblical text with a lifeless monotone voice. Rather, the Hebrew word for "read" (קָרָא) means "to call, proclaim."[36] It is the same word used to describe the fiery proclamation of Jonah in Nineveh when he "cried out" to the people (Jon. 3:4). It signifies the passionate delivery of the truth marked by a full conviction, deep feeling, and zealous intensity by the preacher.

This is precisely how Ezra read the Scriptures. Ezra took

great pains to give the "exact pronunciations, intonation and phrasing, so as to make the units of the piece and its traditional sense readily comprehensible."[37] Bible scholar David Deuel has noted, "Interpretive comments served only to enhance the reading, not the other way around."[38] Thus Ezra read the Word with deep-seated conviction and care.

This practice of the public reading of Scripture is seen throughout the pages of the Bible. For example, Jesus launched His public ministry by reading Scripture. "He came to Nazareth, where He had been brought up; and as was His custom, He entered the synagogue on the Sabbath, and stood up to read. And the book of the prophet Isaiah was handed to Him. And He opened the book and found the place where it was written" (Luke 4:16–17). He proceeded to read Isaiah 61:1–2.

Also, the public reading of the Scriptures was practiced by the apostles. Peter began his powerful proclamation of Christ on the Day of Pentecost by quoting Joel 2:28–32 and then Psalms 16:8–11; 89:3; and 110:1–2. Reading remained the continued apostolic practice in the early church as seen in Paul's instruction to Timothy: "Until I come, give attention to the public reading of Scripture, to exhortation and teaching" (1 Tim. 4:13).

As David Dombek wrote, "One of the most wonderful facets of our duty as proclaimers of the Word of God . . . or in the worship of the Lord is the oral reading of the Word. Through it we proclaim the Word of our Father directly to His people."[39] Unfortunately, the reading of Scripture in worship services today is often relegated to secondary status—if it is even read at all. John Blanchard laments, "There are times when I have thought that the Bible was being read with less preparation than the notices—and with considerably less understanding."[40] And master expositor Stephen Olford once exhorted an assembly of pastors who read aloud the Scriptures: "Read it as though you believe it."[41]

RESTATING THE WORD

As Ezra read the Scripture, he and the Levites with him
explained the text. Thus, Ezra "read from the book, from
the law of God" and was "translating [מְפֹרָשׁ] to give the
sense so that they understood the reading" (Neh. 8:8). Some
scholars are convinced that this denotes only the work of
translation as the Jews, now returning to their land from the
Babylonian captivity, spoke Aramaic and needed someone
to translate the Hebrew for them into their own vernacu-
lar.[42] But this view, Kaiser argues, does not make sense in
light of the fact that at that time other Old Testament books
were being written and received in Hebrew, such as Haggai,
Zechariah, and Malachi, 1 and 2 Chronicles, Ezra, Nehemiah, and Esther.[43] It hardly seems reasonable that these Bible
books would have been written and preserved in the Hebrew language if Hebrew was no longer understood by the
people. Most probably, the Jews in Jerusalem in Ezra's day
could understand enough Hebrew to follow his reading of
Scriptures. As MacLaren observes, "There is no reason to
suppose that the audience, most of whom had been born in
the land, were ignorant of Hebrew."[44] Thus, Ezra's task included more than translation. It was probably primarily interpretation and explanation.[45]

Ezra gave "the sense" of the passage, thus helping his hearers understand the text—"they understood the reading" (v. 8).
Six times this chapter states that the people "understood" or
had "understanding" (vv. 2–3, 7–8, 12–13).

Giving a proper understanding of God's Word is always
at the heart of true Bible exposition, never peripheral to it.
Above all, biblical preaching should give the true meaning
of a passage of Scripture, moving from the original language
in which the text was written to providing a clear understanding in the mind of the listeners, all the while making

personal application that calls for life-changing choices. Stott writes, "With painstaking, meticulous and conscientious care, the Scriptures, the very words of the living God, must be studied and then opened up to others."[46] Haddon Robinson has written, "At its best, expository preaching is the presentation of biblical truth, derived from and transmitted through a historical, grammatical, Spirit-guided study of a passage in its context, which the Holy Spirit applies first to the life of the preacher and then through him to his congregation."[47]

Biblical preaching finds its message originating solely in Scripture, extracted through correct interpretation in which the original God-intended meaning of Scripture is explained and applied to people today. We should remember the telling words of Bible scholar Merrill Unger:

> No matter what the length of the portion explained may be, if it is handled in such a way that its real and essential meaning as it existed in the mind of the particular Biblical writer and in the light of the over-all context of Scripture is made plain and applied to the present-day needs of the hearers, it may properly be said to be expository preaching. It is emphatically not preaching about the Bible, but preaching the Bible. "What saith the Lord" is the alpha and the omega of expository preaching. It begins in the Bible and ends in the Bible and all that intervenes springs from the Bible. In other words, expository preaching is Bible-centered preaching. Whatever extra-Biblical material is employed—illustrations from human experience, history, archaeology, philosophy, art or science—must be purely subsidiary and strictly fitted into one single aim—to elucidate the portion of Scripture chosen, whatever its length, and enforce its claims upon the hearers.[48]

A CLARION CALL TO ALL

Walter Kaiser echoed Unger's words when he wrote,

"Regardless of what new directives and emphases are periodically offered, that which is needed above everything else to make the Church more viable, authentic, and effective, is a new declaration of the Scriptures with a new purpose, passion, and power."[49] This was clearly the pattern demonstrated in the life of Ezra. So it must be with all who preach today.

Kaiser poignantly issues a clarion call to all preachers:

> *Too often the Bible is little more than a book of epigrammatic sayings or springboards that give us a rallying point around which to base our editorials. But where did we get the audacious idea that God would bless our opinions or judgments? Who wants to hear another point of view as an excuse for a Bible study or a message from the Word of God? Who said God would bless our studies, our programs for the church, or our ramblings on the general area announced by the text? Surely this is a major reason why the famine of the Word continues in massive proportions in most places in North America. Surely this is why the hunger for the teaching and proclamation of God's Word continues to grow year after year. Men and women cannot live by ideas alone, no matter how eloquently they are stated or argued, but solely by a patient reading and explanation of all of Scripture, line after line, paragraph after paragraph, chapter after chapter, and book after book. Where are such interpreters to be found, and where are their teachers?*[50]

This is the question of the hour. Where are such expositors? Where are such Bible teachers? These heart-searching questions should rally all who preach and teach to overcome the present dearth of expository preaching.

This present-day "famine" of "hearing the words of the Lord" (Amos 8:11) must be traced back to a famine of preaching the Word. Surely John Stott is right when he observes, "The low level of Christian living is due more than anything else to the low level of Christian preaching."[51] May preachers today expound the Book, the *whole* Book, and *nothing but* the Book—so help them God!

Notes

1. Walter C. Kaiser Jr., "A Call to Renew the Work of God," commencement address, Dallas Theological Seminary, 29 April 2000. See also Walter C. Kaiser Jr., *Revive Us Again* (Nashville: Broadman & Holman, 1999), 166.

2. Merrill F. Unger, "The Need of Expository Preaching in the Twentieth Century," *Bibliotheca Sacra* 111 (July–September 1954): 231.

3. Ibid.

4. James Montgomery Boice, *Whatever Happened to the Gospel of Grace?* (Wheaton, Ill.: Crossway, 2001), 19.

5. Merrill Unger, *Unger's Commentary on the Old Testament* (Chicago: Moody, 1981), 2:630.

6. Derek Kidner, *Ezra and Nehemiah* (Downers Grove, Ill.: InterVarsity, 1979), 62.

7. John Martin, "Ezra," in *The Bible Knowledge Commentary, Old Testament,* ed. John F. Walvoord and Roy B. Zuck (Wheaton, Ill.: Victor, 1985), 666.

8. John N. Oswalt, "בּוּן" in *Theological Wordbook of the Old Testament,* ed. R. Laird Harris, Gleason L. Archer Jr., and Bruce K. Waltke (Chicago: Moody, 1980), 1:433.

9. George J. Zemek Jr., "Aiming the Mind: A Key to Godly Living," *Grace Theological Journal* 5 (fall 1984): 206.

10. F. Charles Fensham, *The Books of Ezra and Nehemiah,* New International Commentary on the Old Testament (Grand Rapids: Eerdmans, 1982), 100.

11. Andrew Bowling, "לֵבָב" in *Theological Wordbook of the Old Testament,* 1:466.

12. Alex Luc, "לֵב" in *New International Dictionary of Old Testament Theology and Exegesis,* ed. Willem A. VanGemeren (Grand Rapids: Zondervan, 1997), 2:749.

13. Charles Spurgeon, *Autobiography* (Edinburgh: Banner of Truth, 1973), 2:159.

14. Leonard J. Coppes, "דָּרַשׁ" in *Theological Wordbook of the Old Testament,* 1:198–99.

15. S. Wagner, "דָּרַשׁ" in *Theological Dictionary of the Old Testament,* ed. G. Johannes Botterweck and Helmer Ringgren (Grand Rapids: Eerdmans, 1978), 3:294.

16. David Denninger, "דרשׁ" *New International Dictionary of Old Testament Theology and Exegesis,* ed. Willem A. Van Gemeren (Grand Rapids: Zondervan, 1997), 1:993.

17. As quoted in Hugh T. Kerr, *A Compend of Luther's Theology* (Philadelphia: Westminster, 1943), 17. All biblical expositors owe a great debt to John Piper for his outstanding research in surveying the personal study of Mar-

tin Luther. See the chapter on Martin Luther entitled "Sacred Study" in Piper's book *The Legacy of Sovereign Joy* (Wheaton, Ill.: Crossway, 2000), 77–111.

18. As quoted in Ewald M. Plass, comp., *What Luther Says: An Anthology* (St. Louis: Concordia, 1959), 3:1359.

19. Ibid., 3:1355.

20. Piper, *The Legacy of Sovereign Joy,* 79.

21. John MacArthur, *The MacArthur Study Bible* (Nashville: Word Bibles, 1997), 638, 649.

22. Fensham, *The Books of Ezra and Nehemiah,* 100.

23. Michael P. Green, *Illustrations for Biblical Preaching* (Grand Rapids: Baker, 1997), 36.

24. "Taking the World's Temperature: An Interview with Billy Graham," *Christianity Today,* 23 September 1977, 19.

25. Mervin Breneman, *Ezra, Nehemiah, Esther,* New American Commentary (Nashville: Broadman & Holman, 1993), 129–30.

26. Eugene Carpenter, "עשׂה" in *New International Dictionary of Old Testament Theology and Exegesis,* 3:546.

27. As quoted in John Blanchard, comp., *Gathered Gold* (Darlington, Del.: Evangelical, 1984), 19.

28. As quoted in John Blanchard, comp., *More Gathered Gold* (Welwyn, U.K.: Evangelical, 1986), 213.

29. Ibid., 216.

30. As cited in R. Kent Hughes, *1001 Great Stories and "Quotes"* (Wheaton, Ill.: Tyndale, 1998), 24.

31. As quoted in Blanchard, *More Gathered Gold,* 214.

32. Unger, "The Need of Expository Preaching in the Twentieth Century," 231.

33. John R. W. Stott, "Christian Preaching in the Contemporary World," *Bibliotheca Sacra* 145 (October–December 1988): 364.

34. Charles Haddon Spurgeon, *The Metropolitan Tabernacle Pulpit* (Pasadena, Tex.: Pilgrim, 1975), 35:105.

35. As quoted in J. I. Packer, "Calvin the Theologian," in *John Calvin: A Collection of Essays,* ed. James Atkinson, et al. (Grand Rapids: Eerdmans, 1966), 166.

36. Edwin Yamauchi, "Ezra, Nehemiah," in *The Expositor's Bible Commentary* (Grand Rapids, Zondervan, 1988), 4:724.

37. Michael A. Fishbane, *Biblical Interpretation in Ancient Israel* (New York: Oxford University Press, 1985), 109.

38. David Deuel, "An Old Testament Pattern for Expository Preaching," *Master's Seminary Journal* 2 (1991): 135.

39. David A. Dombek, *Reading the Word of God Aloud: The Preacher and Preaching,* ed. Samuel T. Logan (Phillipsburg, N.J.: Presbyterian and Reformed, 1986), 424.

40. John Blanchard, quoted in Hughes, *1001 Great Stories and "Quotes,"* 24.

41. Stephen Olford, "Why I Believe in Expository Preaching," audio tape of pastors' luncheon message at Dauphin Way Baptist Church, Mobile, Alabama, 22 March 1999. In his book *Anointed Expository Preaching* (Nashville: Broadman & Holman, 1998), Olford noted, "The reading of Scripture is *the most important* part of public worship. Even the sermon must come under the sentence of the Word!" (24; italics in original).

42. Fensham, *The Books of Ezra and Nehemiah,* 217.

43. Kaiser, *Revive Us Again,* 166.

44. Alexander MacLaren, *Expositions of Holy Scripture* (Grand Rapids: Baker, 1984), 3:376.

45. "The basic meaning of the word in question (*meporas*) is 'to make distinct, or separate,' which could denote either that the reading was well articulated or that the law was read and expounded section by section. Either of these would be appropriate, probably both were true" (Kidner, *Ezra and Nehemiah,* 106).

46. Stott, "Christian Preaching in the Contemporary World," 368.

47. Haddon W. Robinson, "What Is Expository Preaching?" *Bibliotheca Sacra* 131 (January–March 1974): 57.

48. Merrill F. Unger, "Expository Preaching," *Bibliotheca Sacra* 111 (October–December 1954): 333–34.

49. Walter C. Kaiser Jr., *Toward an Exegetical Theology* (Grand Rapids: Baker, 1981), 242.

50. Kaiser, *Revive Us Again,* 166–67.

51. Stott, "Christian Preaching in the Contemporary World," 365.

Until I come, give attention to the public reading of Scripture, to exhortation and teaching. Do not neglect the spiritual gift within you, which was bestowed upon you through prophetic utterance with the laying on of hands by the presbytery. Take pains with these things; be absorbed in them, so that your progress may be evident to all. Pay close attention to yourself and to your teaching; persevere in these things; for as you do this you will insure salvation both for yourself and for those who hear you.

1 TIMOTHY 4:13–16

"Preaching is the public exposition of Scripture by the man sent from God, in which God himself is present in judgment and in grace."

❖ JOHN CALVIN

4

NO HIGHER CALLING
THE PASSION OF BIBLICAL PREACHING

JOHN MACARTHUR, highly regarded pastor and author, once told a large group of preachers at a national pastor's conference, "Now is the time for the strongest men to preach the strongest message in the context of the strongest ministry."

That provocative statement reached out and grabbed me by the lapels, drawing me up short in the pew. The words hit me with the force of a devastating knockout punch—the *strongest* men . . . the *strongest* message . . . the *strongest* ministry.

What this gifted Bible expositor said struck me at the core of my being. With great resolve, I determined, *God, I will to be one of those men.* This is the burning passion of my heart. Furthermore, it should be the heartbeat of all who are called to preach God's Word. This is the need of the hour— the strongest men preaching the strongest message in the strongest ministry.

Martyn Lloyd-Jones, the noted pastor of London's Westminster Chapel, once wrote, "The work of preaching is the highest and the greatest and the most glorious calling to which anyone can ever be called."[1] This is true, not because there is anything special about the messenger, but because there is everything glorious about the Lord who summons His men to preach. Because the Bible is the inspired, inerrant, and infallible Word of the living God, the call to proclaim the Word is the highest calling known to mankind.

This high and holy commission to preach requires nothing less than the wholehearted devotion of all who answer its sacred call. Only an absolute abandonment to God's work will successfully fulfill the rigorous demands of biblical preaching. Focused intellect, exhausting study, fervent heart, draining concentration, and long hours are all required to give birth to an expository sermon. So are intense spiritual warfare, personal fortitude, and soul-searching prayer.

As Winston Churchill so passionately offered "blood, toil, tears, and sweat" on his country's behalf, so the preacher must bring nothing less to the pulpit. If his expositions are to infuse divine life into the souls of his hearers, the preacher must abandon his life to this sacred task. Biblical preaching requires the heart, soul, mind, and strength of the one called to preach—the entirety of his life.[2]

Unfortunately, many men enter their pulpits each Sunday without understanding or feeling the eternal weight of glory resting on their shoulders. In what more resembles "sermonettes for Christianettes," casual discourses are becoming increasingly focused on massaging "felt needs" rather than allowing the biblical text to expose *real needs*. In light of this disturbing trend, pastors must return to preaching that is "Bible-based, Christ-focused, and life-changing . . . marked by doctrinal clarity, a sense of gravity, and convicting argument."[3] Passionate, biblical preaching from God-dominated men must be restored to the pulpit.

A DIVINE MANUAL FOR PREACHING

Perhaps no portion of Scripture is more germane to the subject of biblical preaching than 1 and 2 Timothy. Written by the apostle Paul to his young son in the faith, Timothy, these letters provide timeless instruction on how to lead the church and how to preach in a manner that is well pleasing to God. Admittedly, there is room for diversity in preaching according to each person's giftedness, abilities, and personality. Nevertheless, God has provided some basic guidelines in 1 and 2 Timothy that should direct all preaching. One particular passage—1 Timothy 4:13–16—is the focus of this chapter.

The historical background of 1 Timothy reveals that Paul had been recently released from his first Roman imprisonment and had launched a fourth missionary journey to visit several of the churches he had visited earlier, including the congregation at Ephesus. After a brief stay there, the apostle left Timothy with the formidable task of leading this congregation, a troubled church with a number of problems. False teachers in the church were spreading heresies (1:3–7; 4:1–3; 6:3–5).[4] Other problems that existed in that congregation were these: aggressive women were overstepping their God-assigned boundaries for ministry, usurping the headship of the men (2:9–15); unqualified men may have been serving in key positions of spiritual leadership (3:1–13; 5:17–22); people were looking down on Timothy because of his youthfulness and thus challenging his authority (4:12); the care of numerous widows was being overlooked (5:3–16); and many of the wealthy among the congregation were becoming conceited (6:7–11, 17). Regarding these challenges, Kent Hughes concluded, "Timid Timothy was in a tough spot—pastoring a church that had not called him—ministering to a people who despised his youth and inexperience."[5]

When Paul arrived in Macedonia (1:3), he wrote this letter to Timothy, a manuscript with instructions on how to carry out his oversight of the church (3:14–15). Thus, this epistle presents wise counsel from a seasoned apostle on how to lead the church, how to deal with the problems that existed, and even how to preach. The references to preaching and teaching in 1 Timothy are plentiful and overwhelmingly outweigh all other ministry charges given by the apostle (1:3, 5; 2:11–12; 3:2; 4:1, 6–7, 11, 13, 16; 5:7, 17; 6:2–3, 17–18, 20).

This stated preoccupation with biblical teaching and preaching is not surprising because it is to be the nerve center for every church, the chief means of cultivating spiritual life in the body of Christ. First Timothy 4:13–16 is the most strategic passage on the subject of preaching in Paul's first epistle to Timothy, providing valuable insight into the true nature of biblical proclamation. In these verses, Paul called for preaching that is intensely Word-centered and comes through one who is deeply Word-absorbed. In other words, exposition must come from one who is consumed with a fervent zeal for God's Word. The pastor is to be, first and foremost, a *preacher*—a man consumed with a burning passion to study, read, expound, and live the Scriptures.

THE PURSUIT OF BIBLICAL PREACHING

The apostle wrote in 1 Timothy 4:13, "Until I come, give attention to the public reading of Scripture, to exhortation and teaching." In other words, Paul was saying, "Timothy, until I can arrive, pour yourself into one primary task— preaching." Hughes says of this verse: "This simple sentence is a landmark text in defining the major work of the pastor and the worship of the church."[6]

Here is the central thrust of Paul's repeated counsel to Timothy: Preach the Word! The young pastor was to devote himself to this sacred task. Three observations are worth noting about this exhortation.

A CONSUMING PURSUIT

First, the pursuit of biblical preaching should be consuming. The verb "give attention to" *(prosecho)* means to "turn one's mind to" something in order to "occupy oneself with, devote or apply oneself to it."[7] This same word is used in Hebrews 7:13 to depict "the absolute absorption" with which the priest stood at the altar with "all thought and energy taken up with the object."[8] Thus, Timothy was "to apply himself" or "devote himself"[9] with undivided allegiance to this foundational ministry of biblical preaching and teaching.

Paul had already used this verb in speaking of the dangers in Ephesus of people who "pay attention to myths" (1 Tim. 1:4) and those who are "paying attention to deceitful spirits and doctrines of demons" (4:1). In combating these dangers, Timothy was to devote himself to "the public reading of Scripture, to exhortation and teaching." The same is still true today with those who have been called to the pulpit. Their ministry of preaching is to be a consuming pursuit, not a secondary issue. Gardiner Spring, nineteenth-century pastor in New York City, stated, "The great object of every minister of the Gospel ought to be to give the services of the pulpit the pre-eminence over every other department of ministerial labor."[10]

A CONSTANT PURSUIT

Second, biblical preaching must be an ongoing pursuit of the preacher. "Give attention to" translates a present imperative verb, indicating that Timothy "was to continually give his attention to those things. It was to be his way of life."[11] In season and out, this young pastor was to be *always* preaching the Word (2 Timothy 4:2). He was to preach when it was convenient as well as when it was inconvenient ("in season and out of season"), when it was received as well as when it was well rejected. Timothy was constantly to devote himself to proclaiming the Word. Underscoring this very point, Bible expositor Warren Wiersbe wrote, "Ministering the Word was not something Timothy was to do after he had done other things; it was to be the most important thing he did."[12] Before he gave attention to anything, he must devote himself to preaching. This same vigil is absolutely necessary for all ministers today. Men of God are to give themselves fully to their preaching. Nothing less will suffice.

A COMMANDED PURSUIT

Third, biblical preaching is commanded. Issued with apostolic authority, this scriptural charge to give attention to preaching was binding on Timothy's life and ministry, a command to be obeyed. With this imperative, Paul issued God's mandate for this young man's ministry, a mandate that is timeless for all pastors in all places.

Many today, however, wrongly assume that a pastor is primarily a chief executive officer, whose first priority is vision-casting, strategy-crafting, and image-shaping. But this emphasis dramatically opposes Paul's instruction in the Pastoral Epistles in which he emphatically stated that, more than anything else, pastors are to be *preachers*. Such a priority remains by divine mandate to this present hour.

THE REFORMATION OF EXPOSITION

One noted expositor who "gave attention" to biblical preaching was the monumental reformer of Geneva, John Calvin. His passionate commitment to Word-centered, text-driven preaching remains second to none. For twenty-three years (1541–1564), this Swiss pastor carefully expounded God's Word to his congregation. Calvin preached from the

New Testament twice each Sunday, and every other week he expounded portions of the Old Testament each weekday evening. Before this long period of extended ministry, Calvin had been missing from his pulpit ministry, banished on Easter Day 1538 by the Geneva city council. Yet upon his return from a three-year exile, Calvin entered his Geneva church (in September 1541) triumphant and resumed his exposition *exactly* where he had stopped three years earlier —on the next verse. Later, Calvin became seriously ill in the first week of October 1558 and did not return to the pulpit until Monday, June 12, 1559—an absence of eight months. But when he resumed his ministry, he commenced again at *the very next verse* in the Book of Isaiah.[13] He was consumed with a passion for expository preaching.

In fact, Calvin was so devoted to preaching through books in the Bible that his expositional series often took several years to complete. For example, his weekly preaching through the Book of Acts took over four years. He then preached 46 sermons on 1 and 2 Thessalonians, 186 sermons on 1 and 2 Corinthians, 86 sermons on the Pastoral Epistles, 43 sermons on Galatians, and 48 sermons on Ephesians. In his latter years he began preaching a harmony of the Gospels in the spring of 1559 and continued to do so until he died five years later, on May 27, 1564. During this same time he preached 159 sermons on Job, 200 on Deuteronomy, 353 on Isaiah, 123 on Genesis, along with other expositions as well.[14]

John Calvin's meaty sermons were of such substance that his expositions eventually became the basis of his luminous commentaries. Through his pulpit preaching, he produced commentaries on twenty-three Old Testament books (including ten of the twelve Minor Prophets books), a harmony of the Gospels, Acts, 1 and 2 Corinthians, Galatians, Ephesians, 1 and 2 Thessalonians, 1 and 2 Timothy, and Titus.[15] The great majority of this vast, rich legacy flowed out of his faithful expository preaching. Is biblical preaching relevant? When one considers that Calvin's expository preaching dramatically influenced two continents—both religiously and culturally—the answer must be affirmative.

What could possibly be more relevant than the life-changing power of preaching God's Word? The famed Genevan Reformer towers over the centuries as an example worth emulating in the passionate pursuit of biblical exposition.

THE PATTERN OF BIBLICAL PREACHING

Besides establishing the pursuit of biblical preaching, Paul also gave Timothy a pattern to follow in his pulpit ministry. Timothy's ministry was to consist of three parts—the public reading of Scripture, exhortation, and teaching (1 Tim. 4:13). These three components—reading, exhortation, and teaching—are the strong and sturdy pillars on which all biblical preaching should rest. This triad in Bible exposition indicates "a specific and recognized practice in preaching."[16]

READ THE WORD

The four words "public reading of Scripture" render one Greek word, *anagnosei,* preceded by the definite article *teh* and literally should be translated, "the reading." This referred to the public reading of Scripture in the corporate gathering of the church's worship, a practice dating back to the time of Ezra when he read the Scriptures in the revival at the Water Gate in Jerusalem (Neh. 8:1–8). This practice was eventually incorporated in the worship service of the ancient Jewish synagogue (Luke 4:16–17; 2 Cor. 3:14). With the birth of the church, this Old Testament practice of publicly reading the Scriptures was adopted by the early believers in their New Testament worship.[17] The early church also read from the Epistles and the Gospels. In fact, Paul requested that his letters be read to the churches. "When this letter is read among you, have it also read in the church of the Laodiceans; and you, for your part read my letter that is coming from Laodicea" (Col. 4:16). In another epistle, Paul wrote, "I adjure you by the Lord to have this letter read to all the brethren" (1 Thess. 5:27). Clearly, Paul intended the public reading of Scripture to be an indispensable part of the church's life. Also, the book of Revelation was to be read aloud. "Blessed is he who reads and those who hear the words of the prophecy, and heed the things which are written in it; for the time is near" (Rev. 1:3).

The practice of publicly reading the Scriptures—both Old and New Testaments—soon became an integral part of the early church's worship. "Reading Scripture included at the least the Old Testament, but it may have referred also to the rapidly growing collection of New Testament writings."[18] Underscoring the central importance of the Scriptures in the life of the church, Calvin noted that Paul "places reading before doctrine and exhortation; for, undoubtedly, the Scripture is the fountain of all wisdom, from which pastors must draw all that they place before their flock."[19] The preacher, as the worship leader, should follow Paul's instruction to read the Scriptures publicly, and not allow other activities to crowd it out.

APPLY THE WORD

Also, Paul insisted that the reading of Scripture be accompanied by "exhortation." This word "exhortation" (*paraklesis*) means "to come alongside" with the purpose of helping someone who is weak or wayward. Accompanied with a definite article, "the exhortation" refers to a specific element of preaching, which "suggests the applying of the

Word to the lives of the people."[20] This was the practice of the ancient synagogue in which the exhortation followed the reading and "was an exposition and application of the Scripture by way of exhortation or encouragement to a certain course of conduct."[21] For example, in the synagogue in Antioch in Pisidia "the reading of the Law and the Prophets" was followed by a "word of exhortation" (Acts 13:15). Kelly identifies this "exhortation" as "the exposition and application of Scripture which followed its public reading."[22]

This aspect of exhortation in preaching "is an important part of every pastor's duties. He must not only read the Word of God to his people, but also exhort them to obey it."[23] As MacArthur wrote, "Exhortation challenges people to apply the truths they have been taught. It warns people to obey in light of the blessing to come to them if they do, and the judgment if they do not. Exhortation may take the form of rebuke, warning, counsel, or comfort, but always involves a binding of the conscience."[24] That is to say, the ultimate goal of Bible exposition is changed lives. Preaching must do more than simply inform the mind; it must grip the heart and challenge the will. The entire person—mind, emotion, and will—must be impacted. Thus, exposition is not merely for the transmitting of information; it is for the effecting of transformation. It presses for a decision and calls for a verdict.

John A. Broadus, a great trainer of preachers, wrote, "Preaching is essentially a personal encounter, in which the preacher's will is making a claim through the truth upon the will of the hearer. If there is no summons, there is no sermon."[25] All great preachers are strong in this aspect of exhortation and application. R. W. Dale writes of Jonathan Edwards' preaching, "In the elaborate doctrinal part of Jonathan Edwards' sermons, the great preacher was only getting his guns into position; but in his applications, he opened fire on the enemy. There are too many of us, I am

afraid, who take so much time getting our guns into position that we have to finish without firing a shot."[26] *Apply* the
word.

TEACH THE WORD

Preaching must also include "teaching," or, more literally,
"the teaching" (*teh didaskalia),* which refers to the explanation of the biblical text. The public reading of Scripture
should include a careful unfolding of the meaning of the
passage. "Lest it should be thought that careless reading was
enough," Calvin noted that Paul said "it must be explained."[27]
Commentator Craig Keener noted, "As in the synagogue
service both in Palestine and in the Diaspora, public reading of Scripture was central to the service; the reading from
the Law was probably generally accompanied by one from
the Prophets. The reading was then expounded (exhortation and teaching) on by means of a homily on the text that
had been read."[28] In other words, the early church followed
the practice of reading the Scriptures with instruction that
conveyed its God-intended meaning, doctrinal truths, theological implications, and timeless principles. True expository preaching is always doctrinal preaching.

While "exhortation" is more application-oriented,
"teaching" is more doctrine-oriented. The former deals with
the building up of lives; the latter focuses on the establishing of sound doctrine. As Thomas Lea notes, "Teaching
makes an appeal to the intellect and informs listeners about
the truths of the Christian faith."[29] In so doing, the preacher
is to integrate each biblical text with the larger system of
theology and to show "how the particular passage being expounded fits into the full counsel of God's Word."[30] The expositor is to demonstrate how all biblical truth fits together,
conveying, for example, how the Old Testament is fulfilled
in the New Testament, or how Paul harmonizes with James,

or how Matthew complements Luke. All this requires the pastor's personal study in the original languages, historical background, authorial intent, cross-references, cultural background, geography, grammar, literary structure, and systematic theology. Diligent study is entirely necessary if the true meaning of the biblical text is to be conveyed.

BIBLICAL, YET BALANCED

These three elements—the reading, exhortation, and teaching—are essential for true biblical preaching, and they must be balanced with each other. Hendriksen commented, "A minister should strive to effect a proper balance [among] the reading of Scripture, exhorting, and teaching. Some never exhort. Others never teach. And the reading of Scripture is prone to be regarded merely as a necessary preface to what the preacher himself is going to say!"[31]

Certainly the preacher should carefully consider the peculiar needs of his listeners, but all three elements must be present. Such balanced, biblical preaching means "unfolding the text of Scripture in a way that makes contact with the listener's world while exalting Christ and confronting [listeners] with the need for action."[32]

THE PERSEVERANCE OF BIBLICAL PREACHING

No doubt, Satan did everything he could to discourage Timothy from proclaiming the Word. So, Paul wrote, "Do not neglect the spiritual gift within you, which was bestowed on you through prophetic utterance with the laying on of hands by the presbytery" (4:14). The veteran apostle called his young disciple to persevere in his ministry—no matter what! Such endurance in preaching involves several marks: a strong commitment, a spiritual gift, and supportive affirmation.

A STRONG COMMITMENT

Paul commanded Timothy, "Do not neglect the spiritual gift within you," referring to the God-given ability to preach and teach. Used only here by the apostle, this verb "neglect" (*ameleo*) means "to be careless about something."[33] In Matthew 22:5, it is rendered "paid no attention." In essence, Paul challenged this young preacher, "No matter what difficulty is being thrown at you, keep on preaching!" Perhaps Timothy felt he could no longer handle the pressures confronting him in this difficult situation. Or perhaps he was caving in to public pressure and was toning down his preaching. Perhaps he was on the verge of bailing out. Regardless of what might prompt a moment of weakness, Timothy was exhorted to endure faithfully in his preaching.

Every preacher today must exhibit such unwavering resolve to preach the Word, no matter what may oppose him. The commitment must be constant and intentional.

A SPIRITUAL GIFT

Paul encouraged Timothy to persevere in his ministry because he had been given a spiritual gift by God. This spiritual gift was "his teaching ministry, together with the authority and power to exercise it."[34] MacArthur writes, "Each believer's gift is a God-designed blend of spiritual capacities, which acts as a channel through which the Spirit of God ministers to others. Timothy's gift included evangelism, preaching, teaching, and leadership.[35] If one is to persevere in biblical preaching, he must know he has been sovereignly gifted by God to do so. Only then can he preach with a sense of confidence and destiny in his life.

A SUPPORTIVE AFFIRMATION

Paul added that Timothy's spiritual gift "was bestowed upon you through prophetic utterance with the laying on of hands by the presbytery" (1 Tim. 4:14). In a public ordination, elders laid hands on him, confirming that they recognized that he was called and gifted by God to preach. Kent Hughes writes, "Paul charges Timothy to remember that electric moment in the past, somewhere with Paul in his travels when the man knelt, and Paul and the local elders fixed their hands on him, intoning prophecies and prayers about his giftedness and future ministry."[36] Thus Paul was reminding Timothy that God had given him a spiritual gift to preach and other spiritual leaders had confirmed the validity of this gift. For Timothy to bail out of the ministry now or to waver in his preaching would negate his own ordination.

Every preacher can persevere as he recalls the affirmation of others, and ultimately the affirmation of God. Richard Glover has rightly noted, "None is a Christian minister who has not been ordained by the sovereign laying on of unseen hands."[37] If not fully persuaded of God's call and gifting, a pastor may easily become discouraged when tough times come.

ANCHORED TO THE PULPIT

A strong commitment not to neglect one's gift to preach is the sure anchor that holds during the howling storms of ministry. Consider Charles Simeon, an eighteenth-century preacher. Simeon pastored the Holy Trinity Church in Cambridge, England, for fifty-four years and faithfully preached throughout years of immense adversity. Opposition to his preaching did not come from outside the church, but from his own congregation. For the first ten years of his ministry, his obstinate parishioners chained their pews closed so that visitors were forced to sit in the aisles. However, the closed doors of the parishioners' pews were surpassed by the resistance of their hearts as they flatly refused to respond to his preaching. Yet Simeon's steely resolve enabled him to persevere in his biblical preaching. He refused to neglect his ministry of exposition. As he faithfully preached the Word, God eventually prevailed in the hearts of the people.[38]

Such fortitude is a model of endurance for all who preach today. Following Simeon's example, biblical expositors today must determine to preach with perseverance through tough times.

THE PAINS OF BIBLICAL PREACHING

Furthermore, Paul wrote to Timothy, "Take pains with these things; be absorbed in them, so that your progress may be evident to all" (4:15). In other words, biblical preaching, if carried out as God intends, is highly demanding and soul-wrenching.

DEEPLY AGONIZING

In the command "take pains with these things" the verb *meletao* can mean "to take care, endeavor, or to think about, meditate on, plan."[39] Either meaning focuses on the fact that the preacher "must have a single-minded, consuming devotion to his calling."[40] This conveys the idea of always thinking through and concentrating on one's preaching. Paul is saying, "Timothy, do not allow yourself to be distracted from your preaching. Remain focused upon God's Word and what God has called you to do."

Regarding this necessary mental concentration, Charles Spurgeon said, "That which cost thought is likely to excite thought."[41] That is to say, a preacher cannot have a double agenda in the ministry nor be divided in his thoughts. As Paul later instructed Timothy, "No soldier in active service entangles himself in the affairs of everyday life" (2 Tim. 2:4). When in the pulpit, the preacher is to be riveted on the task at hand, faithfully proclaiming the Word. Timothy was to be meditating on the Scriptures constantly, always poring over the Word, ever considering how its divine truths related to himself and to the lives of those to whom he preached.

FULLY ABSORBING

Timothy, also, was to "be absorbed in" his ministry. The word "absorbed" is not in the Greek text, but is clearly implied. Literally, the passage reads "be in them," which suggests "complete commitment" to the ministry.[42] Timothy was to be completely wrapped up in his ministry of preaching, totally immersed in it, burying himself in this sacred task. Later, Paul spoke of elders who "work hard at preaching and teaching" (1 Tim. 5:17). "Work hard" (kopiaō) means to labor to the point of fatigue and exhaustion. An expositor will be consumed with his work of preaching. He is to be totally engulfed in it. Biblical preaching is as much perspiration as it is inspiration. Biblical preaching is like giving birth to a baby every week or sometimes, twice or three times a week, given that great pain is associated with the delivery of both. The demands of preaching is much like a graduate student living in final exam week—every week. The rigors of exposition drains the entire man—mentally, physically, emotionally, and spiritually.

Of this heavy demand, renowned Presbyterian preacher Bruce Thielemann wrote, "The pulpit calls those anointed to it like the sea calls its sailor; and like the sea, it batters and bruises, and does not rest. . . . To preach, to really preach, is to die naked a little at a time, and to know each time you do it that you must do it again."[43]

CLEARLY ADVANCING

Timothy was to "take pains" in his preaching and "be absorbed in it" so that "his progress may be evident to all." The word translated "progress," *prokope,* was used in classical Greek by the Stoics to denote the advances made by a novice in philosophy or ethics.[44] Despite the attacks of Satan to oppose his work, Timothy, the young preacher, was to make noticeable progress in personal godliness and ministry skills so that his "progress" would clearly be seen by all. In other words, his flock in Ephesus should be able to mark his development as a man of God in Christian character and effective ministry so that the people "will cease regarding him as an inexperienced young man whose authority can be discounted."[45] Such growth in spiritual maturity and ability must be evident in every preacher's life.

A POWERFUL AND HOLY PASSION

The preacher's agony and consumption in his work is the norm for ministry, not the exception. A despondent preacher once asked Spurgeon what he must do in order to draw a crowd like those who were coming to hear the master preacher.

"Simply douse yourself in gasoline, strike a match, and set yourself on fire," Spurgeon answered. "Then people will come to watch you burn."

The point was clear. The preacher must be ignited with holy passion for God and be consumed with reaching souls if others are to be drawn to Christ.

In an earlier era, George Whitefield's powerful preaching was stirring the hearts of the people of Britain. When he was preaching in Edinburgh, many in the town awakened at five o'clock in the morning to gather and hear the evangelist. A man on his way to the tabernacle met David Hume, the notorious Scottish philosopher and skeptic. Surprised to see Hume on the way to hear Whitefield, the man said, "I thought you did not believe in the gospel." Hume replied, "I don't, but he does."[46]

When a preacher deeply believes his message, his strong convictions can have a powerful effect on those who hear him. There is no substitute for the preacher being thoroughly absorbed with proclaiming biblical truth.

THE PREOCCUPATION OF BIBLICAL PREACHING

Finally, every preacher must frequently and scrupulously inspect his own personal life, as well as his teaching, if his ministry is to be divinely blessed. Accordingly, Paul concluded by instructing Timothy, "Pay close attention to yourself and to your teaching; persevere in these things; for as you do this you will insure salvation both for yourself and for those who hear you" (4:16).

EXAMINE ONE'S LIFE

Paul solemnly charged Timothy to "pay close attention to yourself" (*epeche seauto*), to be totally absorbed with maintaining a strong spiritual life as he preached. Timothy was to watch over his entire life, specifically to his outward actions, inner thoughts, and unseen attitudes. This call to personal holiness probably refers back to the five marks of godliness that Paul had mentioned earlier (v. 12), in which Timothy was to be an example in speech, conduct, love, faith, and purity. As Bible commentator Ralph Earle points out, "No matter how straight a person may be in his doctrine or how effective he may be in his teaching, if there is a flaw in his inner or outer life, it will ruin him."[47]

Every preacher must model his message. Just as pure water cannot flow through a rusty pipe and remain clean, neither can the pure truth of God's Word flow through the corrupt life of the preacher and remain a clear message. Donald Grey Barnhouse once exclaimed, "The man who is to thunder in the court of Pharaoh with an imperative 'Thus saith the Lord!' must first stand barefoot before the burning bush."[48] What Barnhouse was saying is true: The character of the message flows from the character of the messenger. The preacher must stand on holy ground before he can speak with holy boldness. If the truth has not impacted the preacher, he cannot expect it to impact others. Echoing this very point, Robert Murray McCheyne once said, "The greatest need of my people is my personal holiness."

ESTABLISH ONE'S DOCTRINE

In inspecting his own life, each preacher must establish and be assured of having right doctrine. Timothy was to "pay close attention to [his] teaching," meaning he must give strict attention to his doctrine, being careful to handle correctly the Word of God (2 Tim. 2:15). The message, as well as the man, must be right if the ministry is to succeed.

Both the character of his life and the content of his preaching must be true to the Lord. "His private life and public ministry" must not be separated. Timothy "was to keep a sharp eye on both, persevering in the instructions Paul had offered in the two realms."[49] To emphasize this further, Paul added that Timothy must "persevere in these things." The Greek word for "persevere" (*epimeno*) means to "to stay, remain in a place, to persist, continue in something."[50]

Paul was saying that Timothy should continually be evaluating his life so that both aspects—his life and teaching —might maintain a right course. Sound doctrine is essential for great preaching. As Martyn Lloyd-Jones said, "Preaching is theology coming through a man who is on fire."[51] Such a relentless examining of one's doctrine is absolutely necessary if one's preaching is to be dynamic.

ENSURE ONE'S GROWTH

Furthermore, Paul challenged Timothy, "As you do this you will insure salvation . . . for yourself" (1 Tim. 4:16). As Timothy persevered in personal holiness and sound doctrine, he would grow in the grace and knowledge of Jesus Christ. Not to be misunderstood, this does not mean Timothy would save himself from eternal condemnation through his good works, but his personal godliness and sound preaching would stimulate his spiritual growth. His constant oversight of himself would produce godliness and give "incontrovertible evidence"[52] of his salvation. In keeping with this, Spurgeon believed more strongly in preparing himself than even in preparing his sermons—a necessary reminder for all who preach.[53] Only by living a changed life can a preacher deliver a life-changing message.

EDIFY ONE'S LISTENERS

Moreover, Paul added, "As you do this you will insure salvation . . . for those who hear you." In other words, Timothy's faithfulness in living and preaching the Word would be greatly used by God to produce the same commitment in his hearers. Paul viewed Timothy as "an effective agent under God in the salvation of men."[54] Of course, Timothy himself could not save anyone. But God would use his example and expositional preaching to bring sinners to faith in Christ, as well as to bring saints to greater maturity in Him. If Timothy would examine his own life and ministry, faithfully preaching the Word, he could expect to see others saved through his ministry, as well as people growing in spiritual maturity. Thus, the preacher's goal is the changed lives of those to whom he preaches. As Puritan Thomas Manton said, "The hearer's life is the preacher's best commendation."

HOLDING FORTH THE TORCH OF TRUTH

Biblical preaching must come from the life of one who is fervent for the glory of God, zealous for the Word of God, and aflame for the souls of men, women, and youth. In a word, the expositor must be *passionate*. "Nothing," Richard Baxter said, "is more indecent than a dead preacher speaking to dead sinners the living truth of the living God."[55] "Dispassionate preaching is a lie," R. C. Sproul argues, for "it denies the very content it conveys."[56] But when the truth is preached through one who is fully absorbed in God's Word, the ministry will be wonderfully blessed by God, ensuring the salvation of those who sit under its exposition.

On the last evening of his earthly life, George Whitefield began to mount the stairs of the Presbyterian manse at Newbury Port, Massachusetts, where he was staying on a preaching expedition. His tireless schedule had taken its toll on this aging evangelist. As he ascended the stairs, the townspeople came pressing at the door, longing to hear the gospel from his lips once more. Now fifty years of age, he was weakening, worn out from a lifetime of evangelistic labors. For days he had been so infirm that he should not have left his bed, but he did, all to preach again. At the crowd's insistence, the weary evangelist began to expound the Scriptures. There he stood, candle in hand, preaching with renewed zeal, unaware of the passing time, until the flame finally burned itself out, leaving the room in darkness. The sermon was over, and Whitefield dismissed the crowd. No one knew it at the time, but that was the last sermon Whitefield would preach. Later that night, the gifted evangelist who was used so mightily by God to help usher in the Great Awakening entered into his heavenly rest.

The burning candle Whitefield had held was representative of his life and ministry. It had been a blazing torch that had burned brightly in a dark generation, shining forth the brilliant light of divine truth, faithful until the end. But finally, as with every preacher, it burned its last.[57] Whitefield died as he had lived, relentlessly preaching the Word, holding forth the light of the glory of God in Christ.

George Whitefield's tireless perseverance should inspire all today who are called to preach. May the holy flame of each God-called preacher burn brightly in this dark hour, faithful to the end.

Notes

1. Martyn Lloyd-Jones, *Preaching and Preachers* (Grand Rapids: Zondervan, 1971), 9. Reflecting on the promising medical career that he gave up to enter the ministry, Lloyd-Jones once commented, "I gave up nothing; I received everything. I count it the highest honor that God can confer on any man to call him to be a herald of the gospel" (quoted in R. Kent Hughes, *1001 Great Stories and "Quotes"* [Wheaton, Ill.: Tyndale, 1998], 329).

2. For a further discussion of these rigorous demands, see Peter Adam, *Speaking God's Words: A Practical Theology of Expository Preaching* (Downers Grove, Ill.: InterVarsity, 1996), 157–73.

3. Alistair Begg, *Preaching for God's Glory* (Wheaton, Ill.: Crossway, 1999), 11.

4. For a discussion of this heresy see David A. Mappes, "The Heresy Paul Opposed in 1 Timothy," *Bibliotheca Sacra* 156 (October–December 1999): 452–58.

5. R. Kent Hughes and Bryan Chapell, *1 and 2 Timothy and Titus* (Wheaton, Ill.: Crossway, 2000), 119.

6. Ibid., 115.

7. George W. Knight III, *The Pastoral Epistles: A Commentary on the Greek Text, New International Greek Testament Commentary,* U.K. (Grand Rapids: Eerdmans, 1992), 207. See *prosecho.*

8. James Allen, *What the Bible Teaches* (Kilmarnock, United Kingdom: John Ritchie, 1983), 8:242.

9. Ralph Earle, "1 Timothy," in *The Expositor's Bible Commentary* (Grand Rapids: Zondervan, 1978), 11:374.

10. Gardiner Spring, *The Power of the Pulpit* (London: Banner of Truth, 1986), 109.

11. John MacArthur Jr., *1 Timothy* (Chicago: Moody, 1995), 175.

12. Warren W. Wiersbe, *The Bible Exposition Commentary* (Wheaton, Ill.: Victor, 1989), 2:227.

13. Geoffrey Thomas, "The Wonderful Discovery of John Calvin's Sermons," *Banner of Truth,* January 2000, 22.

14. John Piper, *The Legacy of Sovereign Joy* (Wheaton, Ill.: Crossway, 2000), 139.

15. MacArthur, *1 Timothy,* 177.

16. Allen, *What the Bible Teaches,* 8:242.

17. John R. W. Stott, *Guard the Truth: The Message of 1 Timothy and Titus* (Downers Grove, Ill.: InterVarsity, 1996), 121. George W. Knight writes, "Both refer to public reading of Scripture in a religious gathering, specifically to the reading of the Old Testament in the synagogue" (*The Pastoral Epistles,* 207).

18. Thomas D. Lea and Hayne P. Griffin, *One, Two Timothy, Titus* (Nashville, Broadman, 1992), 138.

19. John Calvin, *Calvin's Commentaries* (reprint, Grand Rapids: Baker, 1984), 11:115.

20. Wiersbe, *The Bible Exposition Commentary,* 2:227.

21. Allen, *What the Bible Teaches,* 8:243.

22. J. N. D. Kelly, *A Commentary on the Pastoral Epistles,* Black's New Testament Commentaries (London: Adam & Charles Black, 1963), 105.

23. Earle, "1 Timothy," 374. Lea reinforces this idea when he notes that this word "includes moral instruction that appeals to the will" (Lea, *1, 2 Timothy, Titus,* 138).

24. MacArthur, *1 Timothy,* 176.

25. John A. Broadus, *On the Preparation and Delivery of Sermons* (New York: HarperSanFrancisco, 1979), 165.

26. As cited in John Stott, *Between Two Worlds* (Grand Rapids: Eerdmans, 1982), 250.

27. Calvin, *Calvin's Commentaries,* 11:115.

28. Craig S. Keener, *The IVP Bible Background Commentary: New Testament* (Downers Grove, Ill.: InterVarsity, 1993), 615. I. Howard Marshall notes that this teaching "may . . . have been based on what was read, but may also be more independent instruction." (I. Howard Marshall, *The Pastoral Epistles,* International Critical Commentary [Edinburgh: Clark, 1999], 563).

29. Lea, *1, 2 Timothy, Titus,* 138.

30. Ibid.

31. William Hendriksen, *1 Timothy, 2 Timothy, Titus,* New Testament Commentary (Grand Rapids: Baker, 1957), 158. Marshall writes, "Timothy is to summon his hearers, to respond to the Scripture that has been read. Whether he does so in exhortation or in comfort will depend on the message of the passage, but common to these two senses is the noted encouragement" (*The Pastoral Epistles,* 208).

32. Begg, *Preaching for God's Glory,* 23.

33. Earle, "1 Timothy," 374. See *ameleo.*

34. Stott, *Guard the Truth,* 122.

35. MacArthur, *1 Timothy,* 179.

36. Hughes and Chapell, *1 and 2 Timothy and Titus,* 117.

37. As quoted in John Blanchard, comp., *Gathered Gold* (Darlington, Del.: Evangelical, 1984), 235.

38. R. Kent Hughes, "Restoring Biblical Exposition to Its Rightful Place: Ministerial Ethos and Pathos," in *Reforming Pastoral Ministry,* ed. John H. Armstrong (Wheaton, Ill.: Crossway, 2001), 91–92.

39. Marshall, *The Pastoral Epistles,* 570.

40. MacArthur, *1 Timothy,* 180.

41. As quoted in Blanchard, comp., *More Gathered Gold,* 241.

42. Marshall, *The Pastoral Epistles,* 570.

43. As quoted in Ben Patterson, "Heart and Soul," *Leadership Journal,* Winter 2000, 122.

44. Kelly, *A Commentary on the Pastoral Epistles,* 109. See *prokope.*

45. Ibid., 108–9.

46. Cited in Clarence Edward Macartney, *Preaching without Notes* (Grand Rapids: Baker, 1974), 228.

47. Earle, "1 Timothy," 375.

48. As quoted in Hughes, *1001 Great Stories and "Quotes",* 329.

49. A. Duane Litfin, "1 Timothy," in *The Bible Knowledge Commentary, New Testament,* ed. John F. Walvoord and Roy B. Zuck (Downers Grove, Ill.: Victor, 1983), 741.

50. Marshall, *The Pastoral Epistles,* 571.

51. As quoted in Blanchard, *Gathered Gold,* 241.

52. Lea, *1, 2 Timothy, Titus,* 141.

53. Ernest W. Bacon, *Spurgeon: Heir of the Puritans* (Arlington Heights, Ill.: Christian Liberty, 1996), 75.

54. Allen, *What the Bible Teaches,* 8:246.

55. As quoted in Charles Bridges, *The Christian Ministry* (London: Banner of Truth, 1967), 318.

56. R. C. Sproul, *The Preacher and Preaching,* ed. Samuel T. Logan Jr. (Phillipsburg, N. J.: Presbyterian and Reformed, 1986), 113.

57. Arnold Dallimore, *George Whitefield* (London: Banner of Truth, 1989), 37.

INDEX OF SCRIPTURE

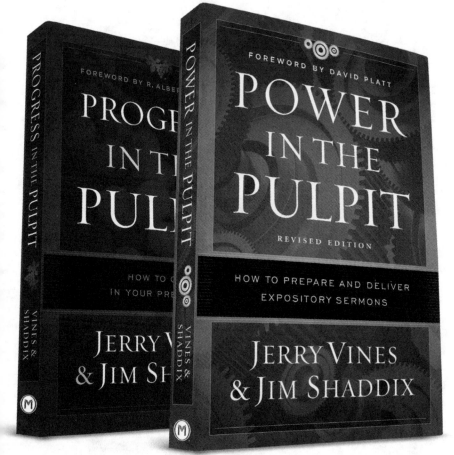

LEEMAN'S CLASSIC BOOK
REVERBERATION IS NOW...

**MOODY
Publishers®**

From the Word to Life®